CORFU

the island of the Phaeacians

EDITIONS
TOUBI'S
ΕΚΔΟΣΕΙΣ

First page: Magical Pontikonisi
and Panagia Vlacherna.

© Copyright   MICHAEL TOUBIS PUBLICATIONS S.A.
                  Nisiza Karela, Koropi, Attiki, Telephone: +30 210 6029974,
                  Fax: +30 210 6646856, Web Site: http://www.toubis.gr

ISBN: 978-960-540-948-7

Contents

Map of the island: Inside cover / Urban map: Inside back cover.

It is full of beautiful trees - pears,
pomegranates, and the most delicious apples.
There are luscious figs also, and olives in full growth.
The fruits never rot nor fail all the year round,
neither winter nor summer,
for the air is so soft that a new crop ripens
before the old has dropped.

Pear grows on pear, apple on apple, and fig on fig.

Homer, The Odyssey, *Book 7. 114-121*

Corfu is the emerald isle of the Ionian, upon which
nature has generously bestowed spots as beautiful as
Pontikonisi. Thick greenery crowds down to the shores
of harmonious and quiet bays and golden beaches,
while picturesque Venetian villages emerge from forests
of olive trees.
Corfu is a miniature earthly paradise.

Corfu has a rich mythology and history, lofty examples
of its arts and culture. Each feature of its natural beauty
is closely bound to the legends and historical events that
have occurred there.

It has received the praises of the likes of Homer and
Xenophon, Casanova and Boundelmonti, not to mention
contemporary artists from all over the world who have
fallen in love with it and recorded its unique beauty and
picturesqueness in works that have a special place in
worldwide literature, painting and copperplates. It was
a bone of contention between the English, French and

Venetians who all passed through and left their mark. The history of the island is like a painting in itself where each culture has left its own special "stroke" of color but where the one overriding fact is the unquenchable and vibrant spirit of the Ionian islands.

A commercial and supply depot of yesteryear, because of its strategic position between East and West, it is not just a way-station of peace and relaxation, but also a place to have a wonderful time with all the delights of a cosmopolitan life.

Corfu is full of mythical landscapes and historical monuments which lead one on tours that have a fantasy element, almost magical. Taking into account the stone boat of Odysseus and the ancient temples, the monument to Menecrates and the Byzantine Angelokastro, not to mention the Venetian garrisons and the western style buildings that grace the town, the fortunate visitor sees stretching out before him the history not only of the island but of Europe itself, of its kings and queens, of its panorama of regimes and cultures, clearly imprinted on the land and the people of Corfu.

Together with that rare feeling for the joy of life and a passion for poetry and music, hospitality has been a sacred duty since ancient times and the desire to offer someone something in friendship is a special trait of the Corfiot.

Nature and tradition that spans the ages calls us to the land of the Phaeacians.

A trip in a carriage from Spianada to the port, in Corfu old town.

Geography

Position
Physical
Characteristics
Geology

Corfu lies on the northern tip of the Ionian sea, at the entrance to the Adriatic sea, a true crossroads between East and West. It is the second largest island in the Ionian complex of islands (the largest being Cephalonia). Together with the Diapontia islands (Othonoi, Ereikousa, and Marthaki), to the northwest and then Paxoi and Antipaxoi to the southeast it forms its own special prefecture. It has an area of approximately 592 sq. km. It is sixty kilometers long while its width varies between 4 -30 kms. Its lavishly diversified coastline has a total length of 217 km.

The Sea of Corfu extends between the island and the opposite coasts of Epirus. The northern secton forms the straits of Ayios Stephanos (2 km. wide). The opening to the south is up to 10 km. wide. From north to south the coastline is uneven. The main harbors are at Ypsos, Garitsa, the salt lake of Chalkiopoulos (where the picturesque Pontikonisi is located), Mantoukios which is also the island's main point of anchorage, to name but a few. The uneven coastline has assisted in the formation of a variety of capes and headlands such as at Ayia Aikaterini (to the north), Kefali (on the west coast facing Italy) and Cape Asprokavos and Lefkimmi (to the south). Corfu is surrounded by a number of small islets. The most important of these is Vido (ancient Ptychia), the old Lazzareto, the former quarantine station (Ayios Georgios), and the charming Pontikonisi.

Between the mountain ranges can be found the meadow-like valley of Roda and the valley in the region of Lefkimmi to the south where there is also the most important lake, at Koryssia. Since it is not large and since the land forms no major mountain ranges, Corfu has no important rivers. However, the regular and heavy rains during the winter months form various torrents: Messogis, Megalopotamos, Gastouri and others.

Geologically, the island is very similar to the mainland opposite which it was once connected to but later split apart from due to a series of major geological upheavals. The Diapontia islands are its extension to the north while to the south one finds Paxoi and Antipaxoi. The land is by and large mountainous. The island is traversed by three minor mountain ranges. The most northerly and widest part of Corfu is covered by the highest mountain range, crowned by Mt. Pantokratoras at 914 m., Stravoskiadi at 849 m. and Vigla at 782 m.

Average temperature in degrees Celsius in the summer months

	May	June	July	August	September
Daytime temperatures	22	32	36	33	24
Night-time temperatures	15	20	24	22	16
Potential rain	4	3	1	0	5

Climate

The thickness of the vegetation and the great variety in color and species is due to the island's mild climate and the large amount of rainfall, and subsequent humidity, unusual for Greece. During the summer the heat is tempered by the moist air while the winters are mild with an average low temperature in January of only 10 degrees Celsius. The *maistros*, a north-westerly wind, blows in the summer afternoons, although it rarely exceeds Force 4. The winds during the winter months are southerly and do not exceed Force 8.

The fossils

For fossil and geology enthusiasts, the Corfu island complex is a virgin paradise. Mount Pantokrator, in particular, with its height of 914 metres, is a 'geological window' over the southern Balkans, with poignant and surprising views.

At Sidari (below) and Palaiokastritsa (above) you can get a clear idea of the island's geological terrain.

Flora Fauna

Corfu, Paxoi and the Diapontia islands, with their 6000 rare species of wild flowers, 55 species of wild orchids and dozens of species of aromatic and medicinal plants, have the most luscious flora of all the Mediterranean islands and provide a true paradise of natural riches. The abundance and variety of the flora and fauna is due to the humid, warm climate, the regular rainfalls, the soil conditions and the islands' geographical location, which attracts plants from Europe and Africa.

In the spring the islands look like boundless gardens full of flowers. The first wild orchid, the Robert's Barlia (*Barlia robertiana*), blossoms in mid-February, whilst the region is flooded with the *Anthemia chamomila* (medicinal chamomile) in early spring. In the autumn we encounter wild cyclamens, the Viola odorata sweet violet, the *Narcissus tazetta daffodil*, the *Iris unuicularis*, the Sternbergia lutea daffodil, the crocuses *Crocus bowles, Crocus pickwick, Crocus longiflorus* and many more. From the sandy coasts with the P*ancratium maritimum* lily as far as the cracks in the rocks on steep Mount Pantokrator, Corfu offers lovers of nature and wild flowers a great variety of beautiful and rare plants that you will not find on any other Mediterranean island.

The vegetation of Corfu has been determined not by soil or climate conditions but by the human factor. The Venetians prioritised the planting of olive trees, and the wild olive became cultivated. The cultivation of vine groves was also important. The olive tree, however, has pride of place in the island's vegetation: infinite olive groves, literally

Wild orchids.

Lilies.

Crocuses.

forests full of eternal olive trees with imposing tall trunks can be found scattered throughout the island. Plenty of cypress trees and a number of palm trees and bushes give the landscape a dense appearance. The cultivable areas cover 65% of the island's total surface, whilst 59% of the cultivated areas have olive trees, citrus fruits, fruit and vines.

With a verdant environment and over 400 species of flowers a large number of colourful butterflies is only to be expected. One common butterfly observed in the summer months is the *Scarce swallowtail*. Of the many reptiles, mention must be made of the Caspian turtle (*Mayremys caspica*), considered rare, as well as the stellion or agama (*Laudakia stellio, Agama stellio*), which is the only European representative of the tropical lizard and is a protected species. Last but not least, is the European otter (*Lutra lutra*), a small animal that lives on the banks of mountain rivers and lakes but only where the waters are very clean. Greece is home to one of its densest and most widespread European populations. An isolated population can be found in Corfu, at the Antinioti Lagoon. The European otter has disappeared from most of its biotopes. As this species is an important indicator of water health it is strictly protected in all European Union nations.

Over 150 species of birds have been recorded in the rich bird fauna of Corfu, many of which are rare and they either live here or pass through the island during migration. The glossy ibis (*Plegadis falcinellus*), Eurasian spoonbill (*Platalea leucorodia*), gull-billed Tern (*Gelochelidon nilotica*), great egret (*Egretta alba*), pygmy cormorant (*Pygmaeus phalacrocorax*), grand cormorant (*Carbo phafacrocorax sinensis*), Eurasian wigeon (*Anas penelope*), Eurasian coot (*Atra fulica*) and the common kingfisher (*Alcedo atthis*) are just some of these.

Common kingfisher.

Water turtle.

Lizard.

European otter.

Natura 2000 areas

Areas that have been included in the Natura 2000 programme and are Sites of Community Importance (SCI) and Special Protection Areas (SPA).

Lefkimmi salt marsh: After 1988 this wetland was used as a salt marsh, and a large and diverse number of changes has taken place since then. Although there is little existing information on its flora and vegetation, which is mainly limited to the sandy coasts, interesting flora and many types of vegetation can be observed here. The region is a refuge not only for bird and animal species but also for several plant species. It is believed that many of the plants that formerly grew in the areas that are today covered in olive groves could survive only in open uncultivated areas, such as this one.

Antinioti lagoon: This lagoon is lo-cated on the north shores of Corfu and is particularly important not only because it is a home to the protected species of the European otter (*Lutra lutra*) but also for the ecological balance it brings to the wider region. The protection and sustainable management of this region is expected to contribute not only to the protection of its wild life but also to its economic development (fishing, recreation, ecotourism).

Korission Lagoon: This region is located on the southwest coasts of Corfu. At the sandy shores located near to the lagoon is the cedar forest, unique to the region, as well as the rock-like sand dunes, which create

View of the Korission lagoon.

an intriguing landscape. The region includes Lake Korission, the largest lake in Corfu, the lake's banks and the areas near the coasts, which are characterised by different types of Mediterranean vegetation. The most important section of this region appears to be the strip of dry land that divides Lake Korission from the sea. This area has a complex and almost untouched ecosystem. As the island's primary wetland it is an important place for the protection of the wildlife and the bird fauna as well as for the preservation of the native vegetation that can be found in the region.

Coastal sea zone from Kanoni to Mesongi: This zone is comprised of stretches of seabed with vegetation (seagrass) and reefs. The water in the region of Kanoni is not deep. The valleys of seagrass extend into the depths of the sea at a distance of 1.5 metres to the south of the village of Mesongi. Here, the seabed is rocky but also sandy, with stones and rocks of all sizes. Seaweed prevails, whilst the bottlenose dolphin (*Tursiops truncates*) can also be found. The presence of the seagrass known as Neptune grass or Mediterranean tapeweed (*Posidonia oceanica*) is of great ecological value. The valleys formed by this species comprise the most important maritime ecosystems in the Mediterranean Sea, contributing significantly to the primary economy.

NOVA ET ACCURATA GEOGRAPHICA TABULA INSULÆ CORFU S...
CONFINIIS SUIS .AC PORTUBUS EX ADVERSO IN GRÆCIA IACENTIBUS

MARE GRÆCUM

MARE ADRIATICUM Vulgo GOLFO DI VENETIA

BOCCA DEL
GOLFO DI
OTRANTO
GOLFO di
TARANTO

VENETIA

MARE
MEDITERRANEUM

S Maura

CEPHALONIA
Insula

Cabo Blanco

BALLIA DI
TOROS

Valle z Stan
Stephan

BALLIA DI
MEZO

CANAL di CORFU sive

Scoglio di Vido als
Macpuro Ins.

Gitadella
di CORFU

EXPLICATIONES

La Sitta di Corfu	O. Opera fatta sotto il Grimani
Fortezza Nova	P. Opra Corna osia fasi nuovo
Scarpone	Q. Citadella
Campana	R. Castiol del Mare
Porte di Basso	S. S. Sidro
Dr. Spilea	T. Campana
Porta Reale	V. Fronte della fortezza Vechia
M. Raimonda	W. Cavallieri
Dr. Raimonda	X. Magazin
Hessa della Sitta	Y. Quartelra
Kavelline fatto sito il Grimani	Z. Progetto di Fortificare la Fortezza vechia in tempo dell afedio
Caponere dentro la fossa aumentia dall afsbriga	a. Portello
Contra mine fatte il Spah	

MARE five CANAL di CORFU seu

CORSULA

MARE

URBS CORFU IN
PLANO EXHIBITA.

te Amsterdam by
JOACHIM OTTENS

SPIANATA

A

TERR

History

Introduction

In Scheria, the island where the mythical Phaeacians lived under King Alkinoos, having settled there from the land of the Cyclopes, according to Homer at least, there developed a highly advanced technological civilisation with boats that sailed on their own without crews, reading the thoughts of their passengers, but there was also a political aspect to this as one finds in the description of the court of King Alkinoos with the superb pieces of sculpture and the lovely plants, which is unique. During historical times the Corinthians founded their own colony on this land which would later wage war against them to achieve their own freedom. The Corfiots held on for over two thousand years against the attacks of the Illyrians, the Vandals, Goths and the occupation of their island by the Romans, Normans, Venetians, French and English.

The fact that this island was able to retain not only its ancient Greek and Byzantine monuments, but above all else the Greek language and traditions, is a historical phenomenon that is rare to find outside Greece. Because ancient Greek civilization was practically the only one to have such a vast political, military and social influence. These are the historical developments that we will be considering in this chapter, which will take us from the depths of time right up to the present.

The names of Corfu

"Makris" ("Long"): because of its long and narrow shape.

"Drepano" and "Drepani": was related to its sickle shape.

Scheria: a) because the goddess Demeter pleaded with Poseidon to stop (schin) the silting up of the river opposite so that the island would not be united with the continental coast, and b) scheros = coast (schein, to have). According to this etymology, Scheria is the continuous coast.

Corcyra (Dorian dialect): comes from an ancient myth connected to the nymph Kerkyra. Kerkyra was a nymph, the daughter of the Asopos river who fell in love with Poseidon. He brought her to this island and gave its name to her. From their love-making was born Phaeacas, the ancestor of the Phaeacians and thus its became known as the "island if the Phaeacians."

Korypho (during the Byzantine period): This name was derived from the "double-peaked" acropolis, which is located in front of the present-day town. From the name Korypho was derived the western Corfou or Corfu (from the latin word Golfo) which is the name the island is known by today to all foreigners.

Copper engraving of the island by R. & J. Ottens, published in 1641-1792. It shows the island itself and the coast of Thesprotia (mainland Greece), together with the Diapontia Islands to the north and Paxi to the south. We are also given an indication of the general area in which the island is set and a diagram of the town with the postitions of its principal buldings.

Mythology

Apollonios the Rhodian mentions in his book *The Voyage of the Argo* that the island was a stopping place for Jason and the Argonauts on their return from their expedition bringing with them the Golden Fleece and Medea. It is also described in the text of *The Odyssey* by the name Scheria. According to Homer, Odysseus after managing to at last escape from Calypso found himself truly on his way home to Ithaca. But Poseidon, the god of the sea, who had borne a grudge against Odysseus since the beginning of the epic, saw his ship and transformed it into a rock. Odysseus was cast into the waves along the coast of Sicheria where he found himself in the kingdom of the Phaeacians, a hospitable people ruled by King Alkinoos. The king's daughter, Nausicaa, went with her maid-servants down to the beach to wash clothes. On the beach she found Odysseus asleep, utterly exhausted. The young maidens sang and played ball and their voices woke him up. Without realizing who he was, they became friends and took him to the palace where he admired the edifices, the harbors, and the beautiful town and was received with full honors. Listening in the palace, to a troubadour singing about the feats of the Trojan War, he was obliged to reveal his own identity and he told the Phaeacians about his various wanderings, and he then resumed his way home at last. According to the legend, Pontikonisi is the boat that Poseidon turned into a rock. But it is not the only place that lays claim to this honor. One of the little islets around Palaiokastritsa is also considered to be the boat of Odysseus. But the beach of Ermones, on the western shore is the most likely place where, according to Homer, Nausicaa met Odysseus.

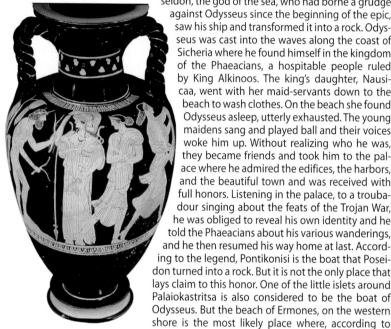

Odysseus under the protective gaze of Athena and holding branches of entreaty approaches Nausicaa, the daughter of the king of the Pheaecians.

Prehistory
First colonists
40,000 BC - 735 BC

The position of Corfu, its wealth and the activity of its inhabitants has made it a center of shipping and commerce since prehistoric times. In any case, from the descriptions of Homer and other ancient writers, one can easily see that the island and the prehistoric town were both thriving long before the events that are known to us now as the Trojan War. Archaeological finds in a cave on Mt. Ayios Matthaios, near the Byzantine fortress of Gardikos have confirmed that the island has been inhabited since the Paleolithic period (70,000 - 40,000 B.C.). On the north coast, at Sidari, have been found the remnants of settlements from the beginning of the Neolithic period. And in the areas of Kefali, Afiona and Ermones settlements from the second millennium B. C. have been discovered (The Bronze Age). The first known Greek settlement on the island was made by the Eretrians from Euboea around 775-750 B.C. for until then the island was inhabited by the Illyrians.

Around 734 B.C. the Corinthians colonized Corfu, in the area around Cape Kanoni. The Corinthian conqueror Chersikratis ruled Corfu with a creative hand and brought it glory and wealth. The Corfiots in league with the Corinthians founded colonies in Epidamnos, minted their own coins and helped spread their influence and the development of their culture even further. Friction did develop between Corinth and Corfu which ultimately led to armed conflict. The naval battle that took place between them in 664 B.C. is the oldest known naval battle between two ancient Greek powers. The Corfiots won the battle against the Corinthian fleet. Soon afterwars, however, they allied with the Corinthians and set out on a campaign to Sicily in order to assist the Syracusans in their fight against the tyrant of Gela, Hippocrates. At the time, Corfu had one of the most important fleets in the then known world.

During the Medean Wars Corfu was considered to be the second strongest naval power in Greece. In the naval battle of Salamis (480 B.C.) the 60 ships from Corfu did not take part due to unfavorable weather conditions.

A few years later, a civil conflict broke out in the Corfiot colony of Epidamnos. The democrats, who had risen up against the oligarchy, sought the support of their mother city. The Corfiots refused and the Epidamnians turned to Corinth. The Corinthians seized the opportunity and sent a garrison to bolster the democratic forces on Epidamnos. The Corfiots were incensed and demanded that the Epidamnians remove the Corinthian force at once. They refused to do that and the Corfiots besieged their town with a powerful force. The Corinthians sent their fleet which engaged the Corfiot fleet in battle at Aktios. The Corfiots proved to be the victors in this battle. The Corinthians did not give in but immediately sent a new fleet. The Corfiots sought assistance from the Athenians who responded with 10 triremes. This naval battle ended with the victory of the Corfiots. The intervention and the contentiousness of the Athenians was one of the main causes of the Peloponnesian Wars.

The figure of a Gorgon on an ancient roof tile from the temple of Hera (Archaeological Museum of Corfu).

In 664 BC, brilliant works were produced on Corfu, under the influence of Corinthian artists, such as the funerary monument of Menekrates, the temple of Kardakios and the temples of Artemis and Hera, with the famous sculptural pediment of the Gorgon. Below, the 7th-century archaic lion that was found close to the tomb of Menekrates.

Drachmas from Corfu,
from the 3rd century B.C.

During that war the Athenians sought the assistance of the Corfiots and they received it. But this only lasted for the opening years of the war because civil strife broke out in Corfu when the oligarchy rebelled, being friends of the Peloponnesians, against the democratic Corfiots. By the time the Peloponnesian War ended Corfu had lost a thousand men and suffered heavy damage and widespread disturbances. Despite all that, the Corfiots managed to live for a few years in peace and harmony and to renew their efforts for a more creative and productive life. In 375 B.C., the Lacedomians launched an attack against Corfu. But with the assistance of Athens, Corfu was able to repulse the attack. Pyrrhos became the new leader of the island and obliged the Corfiots to march along with him on his campaign into Sicily. After the failure of Pyrrhos' campaign Corfu once more regained its independence and resumed its untroubled life.

Recent archaeological excavations have brought to light the ruins of the ancient Roman baths at Benitses in good condition, with their floor mosaics still visible.

Roman period
229 BC – AD 337

And while the roads were opening for a new period of prosperity various neighbors to the north in Illyria as well as the hordes of pirates from all corners of the Mediterranean made many destructive attacks on the island. In the end, the queen of Illyria, Teute, laid siege to Corfu with powerful forces. The islanders, exhausted, finally gave in and surrendered in 229 B.C. At that moment the Corfiots considered the Romans to be their last hope. They addressed themselves to Rome and asked for their protection. The Romans immediately responded. They sent the Counsel Fulvius who successfully liberated the Corfiots. The Corfiots willingly allied with their new friends, who restored a large part of their autonomy and also granted them the right to settle their own highest leader on the island. In AD 337 the Roman Empire was divided for the first time into the Western Roman Empire and the Eastern Roman Empire, with Corfu being part of the Western Empire. The final division, however, came in AD 395, when Corfu was this time included in the Eastern Roman Empire.

Byzantine period
AD 337 - 1204

During the Byzantine period Corfu was unable to retain even a vestige of its former power and vitality. A multitude of barbarian invasions and pirate raids continued to plunder the island's coastline. One of the most important events, was the arrival of Christianity on the island during the first century A.D., brought there by the two disciples Jason (Iason) and Sosipatros who have ever since been paid the highest honors of gratitude by the people of the island.

The Vandals caused serious damage in the 450 A.D. as they carried out repeated raids, not being able to capture the capital, they wrought havoc on the coastal regions and the outlying remote settlements. Justinian's general, Belissarios, made Corfu a base of operations and organized a series of expeditions against the Vandals in Africa and the Goths in Italy. When, however, Belissarios, set off on his campaign to the East, the Goths who had occupied Italy ravaged Corfu and then continued their attacks against other Greek areas, plundering them. For a few years the Corfiots managed to staunch their wounds and apply themselves to an attempt at rejuvenation. They frequently assisted the Byzantines in their campaigns. At the beginning of the 11th century the Normans wanted to use Corfu as a base of operations for their push to the East. The Corfiots rose up in revolt. But the Normans suppressed the rebels with force, defeating both Byzantium and the Venetian fleet which were trying to intervene. In 1147 the Byzantine emperor Emmanuel Komnenos, allied with the Venetian fleet, laid siege to Corfu and in the end liberated it from the Normans.

Four years later the large fleet of the Third Crusade gathered at the island and these Crusaders caused a great deal of damage.

The Byzantine church of Agios Iason and Agios Sosipatros in Corfu town and, above, the icon of Agios Ioannis Damaskinos, a work by E. Tzannes (1682) inside the church.

Frankish and Venetian rule, Angevin rule
1204-1797

When in 1204 the Franks occupied Constantinople, the subsequent division of the Greek spoils left Corfu in the hands of the Venetians. The Venetians then began to organize their new possession.

In 1224 the Greeks under the Despotate of Epirus, led by Michael Angelos Doukas I occupied Corfu and the inhabitants welcomed them enthusiastically. Many of the old privileges of the Corfiot population and clergy were then reinstated. Local tradition attributes the building of Angelokastro to Michael I. Angelus Ducas. The fortress rose on the western coast as a defence against Genoese pirates. The successive rulers of the autonomous region of Epirus granted Corfu the right to keep its privileges, especially the Church, which was recognised as one of the twelve major bishoprics in the Greek world.

When, after the the dissolution of the the the Kingdom of Thessaloniki, the Despotate of Epirus was reconstituted under Emmanuel II, Corfu again became part of this regime (1236). The rule of the Despotate of Epirus ended in 1258 when Despot Michael II Doukas gave Corfu as a dowry to his new son-in-law Manfred, king of the Two Sicilies. Corfu later fell into the hands of Charles I of Anjou (king of the French possession of Naples) and came under **Angevin rule** for the following approximately 120 years (1267-1386).

Silver gigliato of Robert I of Anjou (1309-1343).

Map with the town of Corfu and the two fortress, 1575.

LA CITA DE

Castell Nouo.

Castell Vechio.

LA CITADELA

EL CANALE

During this period the Corfiots suffered much hardship. Charles I was a brilliant ruler but a fanatical persecutor of Orthodox Christianity and the Greeks. He attempted to change the status quo on Corfu in relation to the church, administration and taxation and generally attempted to Latinise the island, with measures so that the whole place would acquire his own ethnic identity. Something like this could not pass, however, and Charles I found himself up against the people and the Church.

After a number of vicissitudes and reversals the Venetians regained control of the island and then stayed on Corfu for more than four centuries (1386-1797). In those four centuries Corfu assimilated its Venetian population and they in return gave the Corfiots many useful elements from their traditions, culture and organisational experience. A significant influence on the later development of the Corfiot economy was the cultivation of the olive which was set down by Venice, under strict guidelines, with punishments

Venetian administration of Corfu

The Venetians based the government of Corfu on the aristocratic model of Venice. Supreme power was concentrated in the hands of the Venetian representatives, although some public posts were given to Corfiot nobles. The inhabitants were divided into three classes, the nobles (Nobili), the city dwellers (Civili) and the masses (Popolari). The education of the working class masses was undertaken by priests in the monasteries, while the wealthier classes had the opportunity to pursue their studies abroad in the universities of Italy.

Angelokastro, the Venetian castle on the west coast of Corfu.

and incentives. This was done so that Venice would have a supply of olive oil which led to the displacement of nearly all other products. The Venetian occupation made Corfu a unique part of present-day Greece, especially since there was no Turkish rule with its concomitant oppression. The absence of a Turkish influence can be seen in every possible way (architecture, town planning, literature, music, life-style) and so Corfu is perhaps to have been truly 'European'.

The Venetians left no monuments or fortifications in Corfu as they did in Crete at around the same period. This was because they felt less at risk from Turks.

The gate of the New Fortress with the lion of St Mark, symbol of Venetian rule.

Napoleon Bonaparte, after he had defeated the Venetians, sent General Gentile to occupy Corfu. With the signing of the agreement the Campoformio recognized the sovereignty of France in the Ionian islands. The French Republicans burned the "Book of Gold" (Libro de Oro) which was the list of the nobles of the island and in its place they symbolically planted the tree of liberty.

The Corfiots welcomed the French with great enthusiasm believing in the proclamations of the French Revolution and hoping that Napoleon would help Greece in achieving its own freedom. In 1798 the French put into operation the first Greek printing shop. But the other great powers of the period (England, Russia and Turkey) did not look favorably at the occupation of the Ionian islands by the French. In 1799 a Russo-Turkish fleet took the island from the French. On 21 March, 1800 Russia and Turkey signed a treaty the terms of which included the name "Septinsular Republic" which was also recognized by the European powers. During this period there was a systematic organization of education, a public library was founded and the first works by Moustoxidis were published on the history of Corfu. The "Septinsular Republic" lasted until 1807. Then, in agreement with the terms of the Treaty of Tilset, a new period of French rule began. For seven years the Corfiots lived with the French in harmony. The French improved the conditions of economic and social life but above all else gave a boost to the local economy through public education. They founded the first Ionian Academy, a model Institute of Sciences

The flag of the Septinsular Republic (1803).

The constitution of the Septinsular Republic (1803).

Autonomous Septinsular Republic

On 24 April 1799, Admiral Ushakov issued a new circular, co-signed by the Turkish admiral, making it known that he was uniting all the Ionian islands into an independent Greek Republic with its own central government and Corfu as its capital. He proposed a senate-led government comprised of the greatest possible representation from all the islands of the new Republic. The constitution of the new state did not differ greatly from that under the Venetians, as it was written by the learned Venetian Angelo Orio, a resident of Lefkada. The constitution was passed without many amendments by the Senate. The Septinsular Republic was immediately recognised as an independent state by all the great powers of the era, even exchanging ambassadors. The new state's only obligation was to pay the Ottomans a symbolic tribute and to have the star and the crescent on its flag. This second obligation was never kept by the Septinsular islanders. Their flag featured a blue background with the lion of St Mark holding the Bible with the Cross upon it in his front right paw and, next to it, seven spears tied together with a band upon which the date 1800 was engraved, the year in which the new state was founded.

and the Arts with an international reputation. The Greek language which had been suppressed was restored with full rights and the Press which had been forbidden by the Venetians, operated with renewed intellectual vitality.

The Ionian Academy (1808)

Many efforts to advance education were made during the subsequent period of French rule. One year after they had settled in Corfu a group of learned Corfiots, in collaboration with French officials, decided to found an academic institution to be known as the Ionios Akademia (Ionian Academy). After a proposal by Donzello, the Ionian Academy was officially recognised by France, with three departments: sciences, ethics and the humanities. This initiative was of no significance for the masses but was highly symbolic in promoting the island on a European level.

British Rule 1814-1864

Liberation from the Turks

When Napoleon fell, the Ionian islands were laid claim to by Austria and England. The Corfiot representative of the Russian empire, John Kapodistrias, set to work to insure the best possible solution. Finally this resulted, in 1815, in the signing in Paris of an Agreement between the representatives of England, Russia, Austria and Prussia. This agreement stated that the Ionian islands would be a free and independent state but under the direct and exclusive protection of Great Britain. The name of the state would be the "The Republic of the Union of Ionian Islands". The peculiar British 'protection' foresaw a military occupation of the islands, approval of the form of government by the British Government and the appointment of a Lord High Commissioner, who would represent the King.

The first British Governor appointed in 1816 was Sir Thomas Maitland. His autocratic and oppressive administration resulted in a storm of protest by the Corfiots and the other inhabitants of the Ionian islands. These protests and the reaction of the local inhabitants soon led to the creation of clandestine patriotic groups. Their mobilization became part of the the the more general revolt of the Greeks during the War of Independence of 1821. Nonetheless, Maitland left Greece its two earliest neo-classical buldings: the Palace of Sts George and Michael in Corfu, which is the largest of its period after the Palace of King Othon (now the Parliament bulding) in Athens, and the Rotonda built in his honour. Generally speaking though, the period of English rule was a dynamic one. They took forward-looking measures for the economy, public health and public education - and for the first time Greek was declared to be the official language -and the Ionian Academy that was founded was to be the first Greek University.

Opposite page, the Ionian Academy and the statue of Ioannis Kapodistrias in Aγios Spyridonas Square.

During the existence of the British Protectorate, a complete road network was built for the island, an aqueduct for the town's water supply was constructed and many civic edifices were erected. The economic life of the island continued to be largely agricultural but there was also a significant development of trade, the arts and letters. In the capital of the Ionian Republic the development of economic life was based, of course, on agriculture and commerce. Its geographical position between flourishing Italy and the ports of the eastern Mediterranean made it a significant depot for international transit trade which was assisted by the fact that there were no tariff restrictions. The last English Governor was Colonel Henry Strorrs (1859). In 1863 the Great Powers signed an agreement stating, among other things, that Great Britain was no longer the protector of the islands. The traty was not, however, entirely favourable, since it provided that the islands would became neutral and that all their

The Palace of St Michael and St George. In front of the main facade of the Palace is the bronze statue of Lord Frederick Adam, one of the best-known British commissioners who built several technical works in the town, such as the aqueduct. The bust is by the sculptor Pavlos Prosalentis, and the gesture of the sculpture's hand towards the water falling into the small lake is a reminder of this excellent technical work that the British commissioner bequeathed to the town.

Ioannis Kapodistrias

(1778-1831)

Ioannis Kapodistrias was the leading figure from Corfu in the 19th century. He studied medicine in Padua but was subsequently attracted to the diplomatic profession, reaching the post of Foreign Minister of Tsarist Russia. In this position, he was involved in drafting the current constitution of Switzerland, with its system of cantons. Kapodistrias was the first (and last) Governor of the modern Greek state, laying the foundations for the great social and political changes of the following generations.

military installations wold be demolished. Thanks to the activoties of Greek diplomats, especially Charilaos Tricoupis, a new treaty was signed the folloing year recognising only Corfu and Paxi as neautral islands. On 21 May the official handover of the Ionian Islands to Greece took place on Corfu. The British left on 21 May 1864 and the Greek flag was raised over the Castle of Corfu, nearly forty years after the liberation of Greece itself.

Turkish acrocities and retaliation for the various unuccessful rebellions brought refugees from Crete, the Peloponnese and Epirus to Corfu as early as the 17th century. As well as swelling the population after the losses of the 16th century, these people made an important contribution to ensuring tha the Corfiots continued to think of themselves as Greek. Despite the fact that Corfu was the seat of the British Administration, and despite the way in which Maitland and his assistants reacted to Ionian Island participation in the 1821 War of Independence, nothing could stop the Greek's struggle for the right to national expression. The Corfios, in the same way as their fellow Ionians, took an enthousiastic part in prepatarions for the uprising and in its execution. The most important personality of Corfiot stock was John Capodistrias, who anandoned a brilliant career in the service of the Russian Empire to play more active part in the War of Independence and to work to make a favourable impression on the Great Powers so that they would recognise the justice of the Greek cause. Capodistrias finally came to Greece and served as the country's first Governor.

Many Corfiots become members of the Society of Friends (the secret patriotic organisation) and were responsible for important initiatives in the preparation for the struggle. Corfiots also served in the 'Secret Band' under Alexandros Ipsilandis. During the years which followed the outbreak of the War of Independence, the Corfiots, whether on their own island, on neighbouring islands, or in other parts of Greece, contributed by assisting refugees, gathering ammunition and supplies for the fighting forces and offering their fortunes and their lives for the liberation of their country. Approximately forty years after the liberation of Greece from the Turks came the liberation of the Corfiots in 1864.

The Prefecture of Corfu was established in 1864, with the union of the Septinsular Islands with Greece. The first prefect of Corfu was Dimitrios-Stephanos Mavrokordatos, whilst amongst those who have served as the island's prefect were Evangelos Averoff and Konstantinos Tsaldaris. For around a century the offices of the Prefecture were housed in the Kapodistrias building, which moved to its own building at 13 Samaras Street in the late 1960s.

The unification of Corfu and Greece signaled a common historical development and indeed the island came to play a major role in the country's political life. Despite all that it's competition with the capital of the country, Athens, was draining. The absorption of its intellectual and economic activities - almost from the very beginning of unification Corfu lost its University - by the end of the 19th century had made the island into your typical provincial center. In contrast to the town of Corfu itself, the rest of the island flourished on both a political and economic level which went in tandem with a growth of population. The increase in the labor dynamic gave an impetus to conversion industry on the island, a broadening of consumer horizons without being incorporated into the more general market of the Greek state which led to a growth of the production of industrial goods and in the end made it a favored location for wholesale production. At the same time the middle class acquired a certain level of economic ease with the systematic use and modernization of the methods of cultivation, increasing agricultural production to the point that in the end this also led to the further support of industrial production. In 1873 the first graphic arts workshop was created on the island. This period coincides with the rising to power of the political circle around G. Theotokis who was Prime Minister of Greece for many years. At the dawning of the 20th century the beautiful island of Corfu found itself on the the verge of new economic and social growth but this time without the cultural emphasis which had formerly played such a leading role. The major world wars had their severe consequences on the island which was crowned by the bombardment and the fires set by the Germans in World War II. Entire blocks, historical and architectural monuments, priceless productions of the spirit and the mind were reduced to a pile of rubble. The first half of the 20th century was hard on the island and new tribulations were faced by the hard-working and patient Corfiots. But the unique natural charms of the island enabled them to overcome these problems once again and to achieve new economic prosperity.

Modern era
from 1864

Kostas Georgakis

During the seven-year period of the dictatorship, from 1967-1974, many Corfiots were part of the resistance. Their only representative on a national level, however, was Kostas Georgakis. The 22-year-old Corfiot geology student, in an act of self-sacrifice and heroism, set himself alight in the early hours of the morning of 19 September 1970 in Matteotti Square in the Italian city of Genoa. This self-sacrifice, a rare phenomenon for the era, shook the world and was considered one of the major acts of resistance. The Republic of Greece and his island of Corfu would later honour the man who gave his life and became a symbol of resistance and patriotism, a forerunner of the sacrifice of the Athens Polytechnic students in 1973.

On 28 April 1941, during the Second World War, Italy occupied the island and ended Greek sovereignty, also making a serious effort to revive the Septinsular Republic with Corfu as its capital. After the Italians had signed a peace treaty with the Allies, the Germans took over the island on 24 September 1943, after destructive battles lasting for many days.

Culture and traditions

Corfu is an island with a multifarious personality. The time-honored love of its inhabitants for the arts and culture in general, its commerce which had made it the second strongest marine power after Athens has today been harmoniously combined with the cultivation of the olive, which was imposed on the island by its Venetian rulers, animal husbandry and last but not least the steadily growing tourist trade which has bestowed its largess upon the island. The unique architectural features of Corfu are at one and the same time an ornament and a historical verification of the life the Corfiots have led during the past few centuries. This is a place more suited the Greek National Anthem than any other being its birthplace really, and music and literature, theater, dance and tradition have survived right to the present with a beauty that is unique and with a special flavor that is peculiar to the Ionian islands. The local customs, with the many western influences which can be found in the music, the churches and even in the island's own special dialect has not changed to even the lightest degree the personality of the individual Corfiot. In the the various religious processions having to do with Ayios Spyridonas (St. Spyridonas), the deeply revered patron saint of the island, in the unique custom of the breaking of clay jugs at Easter, and the ritual of the "First Resurrection", we are dealing with age-old customs which have been preserved, beautiful and moving, and true and which will touch the heart of every visitor. Corfu conveys to the visitor some of the simplest, most genuine and for that reason most beautiful sentiments of its inhabitants but at the same time its desire and almost instinctual longing for singing, dancing and art.

The Corfu of yesterday

In olden times life for the Corfiots was especially difficult. Wages were low, children were plentiful. The villages were smitten with poverty. A little orchard with a goat in it and a labourer's wage in the fields were enough to provide the family's bread but did not always stretch to cover shoes, and so the family would live. The most common food was boiled kale with olives and olive oil. The family would eat its evening meal huddled red-eyed and coughing around the fire which burned in the middle of the beaten earth floor of the kitchen, as the smoke filled the house and slowly filtered out through the gaps vbetween the slates. The kitchen was usually a sort of lean-to bult on to the end of the house.

A large section of the population of Corfu works in agriculture, despite the growth of tourism. The cultivation of the land occupies nearly 65% of the total area of the island. The trees that cover 59% of this area consist of olives, citrus, fruit trees and, of course, vineyards.

The Venetians in their need to secure a sure supply of olive oil for Venice made provisions for the planting of olive trees. This had led to the island becoming an endless olive grove. These ancient olive trees are so densely planted, they are only challenged by the cypress trees. The villagers deal practically the whole year long with the olive trees. and since the trees are so tall it's impossible for anyone to climb them or to even beat the branches with sticks like is commonly done elsewhere but simply must wait for the fruit to ripen and fall on its own. In the villages of Corfu the one unforgettable smell of winter is that of fresh olive oil.

The island's rich flora and cultivation of trees aids honey production, which is a great economic boon for the farmers. Animal husbandry has made Corfu famous for its butter and *graviera* cheese, whilst in the fish-rich marine area to the south of Corfu there is a fishing industry, with lobsters also being caught along the northern and western coasts.

Local cuisine and products

Corfu was a Venetian port for 411 years and it is thus natural that it would have been influenced by Venetian cuisine. With typical Mediterranean ingredients, such as olive oil, vegetables and plenty of herbs, today's Corfiot cuisine displays the diverse influences the island has received. Here we present some typical Corfu dishes. **Pastitsada**: the most popular beef dish of Corfu. Another dish is rooster stuffed with garlic and parsley. **Strapatsada**: thick stock made from bones with butter, eggs, salt, lots of pepper and a few drops of cognac. **Tsigareli**: sautéed wild greens with onions, garlic and spicy red pepper. **Bourdeto**: boiled sea scorpion or school shark cooked in a spicy red sauce, with fresh lemon juice added at the end. **Savoro or Savouro**: small fish marinated in a white sauce with finely chopped garlic, rosemary, vinegar and dark raisins. **Sofrito**: thin slices of fried beef with a white sauce of parsley, white pepper and white wine. **Tsilichourda**: thickly chopped lamb offal with a thick sauce made of plenty of finely chopped spring onions, plenty of pepper and lemon. **Frygadelia**: pieces of lamb liver wrapped in lamb suet sprinkled with herbs and spices. Don't forget to try the traditional desserts of Corfu. **Tiganites t'Agiou,** otherwise known as *loukoumades*, deep-fried pastry dough balls drizzled with honey or syrup and cinnamon. **Sykomaida** or *sykopitta* is made with wine must and dried figs. The **fogatsa** is a type of sweet tsoureki bread of Venetian origin. Finally, despite the fact that the island's vine groves are not large, the Corfiots wash down their meals with excellent **wines**, such as the *kakotrygis* (a white wine with a delicate flavour), *moschato* (white wine with an intense flavour) and *petrikoritho* (a lively red). The island produces its own milk, butter, cheese, yogurt and sausage, famed for its flavor. The "*graviera*" cheese of the island (a delicious delicately salted cheese) as well as its famed "*nouboulo*" (smoked pork filet encased in intestines, somewhat like high quality salami) are unique. There is also considerable production of citrus fruit. But the most famous product is its olive oil.

The **kumquat** is the small Chinese orange that was brought to Europe from Japan in 1846. On Corfu it is used to make a spoon sweet and wonderful liqueur, such as bergamot. The island produces thyme honey, delicious small wild strawberries with a wonderful aroma and a cactus fruit known as **freskamenta** (*pavlosyka* or *frangosyka*). **Mantoles** is a sweet powdered with caramelised almonds and can be found in many patisseries in Corfu town. Finally, you should definitely try the popular **tsitsibira**, otherwise known as ginger beer, made from lemon juice, natural lemon oil, top-quality grated ginger, blonde raisins, water and sugar.

Pastitsada

Ingredients (for 4 people):
1 kilo beef
1 glass olive oil
a little butter
1 large onion
10 cloves of garlic
large ripe tomatoes
1 cinnamon stick
1 bay leaf
salt and pepper
a little vinegar and a little sugar

Slice the meat into small pieces and fry. Remove the meat and fry the onion and the chopped garlic. Add the meat again along with the vinegar and the remaining ingredients and stew at a low heat for about an hour. Boil macaroni (no. 3) in a large, deep saucepan and drain. Put the meat and the sauce in a deep bowl and then add the macaroni.

The kumquat, an exotic fruit with a distinct taste and aroma, has become the island's symbol.

Traditional dances and costumes

The island has a long and rich tradition of folk dancing which began in the mythical times of the celebrations of the Phaeacians and has continued right up to the present with the most expressive Corfiot folk dances renowned for their lively steps, upbeat rhythms and amazing grace.

The major traditional folk dances of Corfu are the 'gastouriotikos', the 'rouga', the 'korakianitios', the 'Ai-Yorgis', the 'mesis' and the 'siniotikos'. They are danced by men and women of all ages, in couples. These dances are a good opportunity to see beautiful Corfiot women wearing there local costumes with charm and pride which are complemented by the special headresses and the unique scarves tied around the waist. The local costume is one of the most interesting folkloric elements on the island and is not only impressive on its own with its vast variety of colors but is further enhanced by various pieces of decoration and jewellery.

There are four types of female costume: 'orous', 'agrou', 'mesi' and 'Lefkimi', called after the different parts of the island.

Male costume does not vary much from one end of the island to the other, and is broadly divided into everyday wear and Sunday best.

A movement from the impressive Rouga dance.

Customs

There are also quite a number of seasonal customs observed connected to the basic tasks of farming (harvesting, grape-gathering and so on) and others related to the daily or festive, occupations of the Corfiot fishermen and farmers. There is also a special custom celebrated on New year's when the locals offer foreigners shoots of basil as a sign of friendship, love and hospitality.

On the **days of the Sts Theodore**, in March, the Corfiots make models of St Theodora and put a water-melon in the place of her head. The water-melon is then shares out amongst those attending the festival.

The **Corfu carnival plays** an important role in the island's traditions, with a history of 450 years and elements that display the strong influences of the Venetian rulers. This great festival begins on Septuagesima Sunday, the ninth Sunday before Easter. The sior Carnival king embodies all the sins of the powers that be and is considered responsible for all the bad things that have happened over the past year. During the central parade, held on the last Sunday of Lent, he is condemned and burnt so that the great party can begin.

The Corfu carnival is especially influenced by the famous Venetian one.

One special custom held on *Tsiknopempti* (Fat Thursday, the last Thursday before Lent) is that of the *Korfiatika Petegoletsia* (gossip). This is a type of street theatre that takes place in the central market of the old town, at Pinia. Amateur actors perform satirical lines in the Corfu dialect, mimicking the ladies who would lean out of their windows and gossip about the neighbourhood as well as other old Corfiot figures. The performances end with the singing of cantatas and *mandinolatas*.

The **Dance of the Priests**, performed on Cheese-Eating Sunday, is opened by the priest who is followed by all the other men in accordance with their position and age and who repeat the lines of the first dancer. The musical instruments remain silent until the elderly ladies arrive, dancing the Corfiot dance.

The **Carnival Wedding** is still performed in the villages of Klimatia, Chlomo, Marathia, Kritika and Lannades. This takes place on the last Sunday of the carnival period and features a mock wedding feast (where both bride and groom are men) which is threatened by the presence of a demon who appears as a satyr.

Varkarola, an impressive parade with cantatas and traditional dances in decorated boats.

The *Varkarola*, held on 10 August, is an impressive custom with a re-enactment of the legend of Agios (Saint) Spyridon, who is said to have expelled the Turks who were besieging the town. During this event lit boats sail up and down the gulf of Garitsa transporting folk bards singing traditional songs to the accompaniment of the guitar and with locals dancing in the boats. The parade ends with a phantasmagoric fireworks display.

At the festival of Corfu you can admire the elaborate decorations of the Corfu costume and the traditional dances full of rhythm.

The festivals of Corfu

The most important feast days, fairs and festivals have a religious origin. Below are some of the most important festivals held during the summer period, from May to September.

1. Easter Friday (Zoodochou Pigis) at Palaiokastritsa.
2. The day of the Ascension at Analipsi and Argyrades.
3. 8 May and 15 August (Dormition of the Virgin) at Kassiopi.
4. 24 June (Holy Spirit) at Kontokali, Argyrades, Stravro, Kastellanous Mesis and Othonous.
5. 29 June (SS Peter and Paul) at Kobitsi, Strongyli and Vitsalades.
6. 2 July (Panagia Vlacherna) with a service at Garitsa and a fair at Acharavi and Kamara.
7. 8 July (St Procopius) at Agios Prokopios and Kavo Lefkimmis.
8. 20 July (Profitis Ilias) at Magoulades.
9. 6 August (Metamorphosis of the Saviour) at Pontikonisi and Agios Matthaios and with a six-day pilgrimage (1-6 August) to the peak of Mt Pantokratoras.
10. 23 August (Panagia Hodegitria) at Gastouri, Peleka and Agioi Deka.
11. 8 September: fairs at Afra, Sinarides, Marathia, Agios Markos and Potami Lefkimmis.
12. 14 September: Feast of the Cross at the Monastery of Agios Ioannis and at Sidari.

Cultural events

The cultural association of Arilla organises the two-day cultural festival **Days of Wine and Culture** every September, with traditional wine-making, music and dance groups from all over Greece.

Corfu International Music Festival.

The **Sardine Festival** is held at Benitses within the first ten days of August. Huge quantities of sardines are cooked on the day of the festival and offered for free to all guests, to be enjoyed to the accompaniment of traditional music bands and partying until the early morning hours.

Ionian Concerts, the Corfu International Music Festival: each summer the Department of Music of the Ionian University organises the Summer Academies. These provide intensive lessons, with seminars and lectures, in arts and music taught by excellent musicians from around the world. The annual Corfu International Music Festival aims to showcase not only the wealth of local music but also to incorporate modern musical thinking into a festival environment. The Ionian Concertos, of an especially high standard, are held each summer as part of this important musical gathering. The concerts are performed in special historical areas of Corfu town, such as the church of Saint George in the Old Fortress, Dimarchiou (Town Hall) Square, the ceremonial hall of the Ionian Academy and Agios Spyridon Square.

International Philharmonic Festival of Corfu: The first International Philharmonic Festival in Greece took place on Corfu in the summer of 2005. A large number of orchestras from Greece and abroad participate as do, naturally, all the philharmonic orchestras of Corfu, with over 1300 musicians taking part.

Be There! Corfu Animation Festival: this is the first international animation festival and, with Corfu at its centre, will be a meeting

info

Department of Music,
Ionian University
Old Fortress, Corfu
Tel. 26610 87504,
26610 87524
Fax. 30 26610 26024,
30 26610 87570
e-mail: music@ionio.gr
Ionian Concerts Festival:
email: info@corfufestival.gr.
www.corfufestival.gr

place for artists from all over the world with competitive activities. The Festival includes film screenings, dedications, original thematic programmes and speeches. The competitive activities are an important element, as is the Kids, Be there! programme, with classes and activities for children (for more information: www.betherefest.gr).

Cultural organisations of Corfu

Kerkyraiki Skini: founded in 1970, the Kerkyraiki Skini (Corfu Stage) has produced over 47 Greek and foreign plays. It has been honoured at many theatre festivals, winning prizes. In 1998 it opened the Polytechno, its own theatre with seating for 75, at 39 Scholemvourgo Street. The Paidiki Skini (Children's Stage) is a department of Kerkyraiki Skini.

Corfu Dance Theatre: Founded in 1970, with its dance company it has participated in numerous festivals within Greece and abroad, receiving excellent reviews. In the past few years the Corfu Dance Theatre has focused on folklore research (costumes, dances, etc.). It is a member of the International Organization of Folk Art (IOV), which is based in Austria, as well as of the Greek section of the IOV, which is based in Athens.

Phaiakes: Founded in 1989. In the past few years it has produced original works with a particular emphasis on Ionian Island culture and tradition (Solomos, Theotokis, demotic songs, etc.). Alongside its theatre workshop there is also a shadow puppet team, which gives many traditional *karakiozis* performances to young and old lovers of this most popular form of Greek theatre.

Corfu Municipal Choir: since 1991 until today the Corfu Municipal Choir has staged operas such as *Norma* by Bellini, *Cavalleria Rusticana* by Mascagni, *La Martire* by Spyros Samaras, *The Murderer's Daughter* by Roboti, *The Godson* by Sakkelarides and Verdi's famous opera *La Traviata*. It also gives concerts with pieces from opera as well as complete symphonic works.

Corfu Choir: founded in 1981 with 500 members. The Choir has performed at many concerts throughout Greece and abroad, participating in international festivals and forums. They have also sung in St Peter's Square in Vatican City, in the presence of the Pope. Their repertoire covers a musical journey, with songs that are pre-classical, classical, opera, musicals, cantatas and contemporary standards.

Corfu Cantata: founded in 1954 by Corfiot musicians and choir singers. It is one of Corfu's three oldest music and dance companies and is maintained primarily by its approximately fifty singers and musicians. It is comprised of the choir and *mandinolata* with guitars and accordion. The Corfu Cantata has performed at many concerts and festivals in Greece and abroad.

Department of Music, Ionian University: the Department was founded in 1992 with the aim of perfecting musical studies, and with the goal of promoting Greek, Byzantine and demotic music and the teaching of contemporary music technology applications. The students of the Department of Music give recitals at places where until recently only the Philharmonic orchestras and choirs performed, reviving the pioneering musical spirit of Corfu.

Corfu Music Conservatory: founded in 1894 with the main aim of teaching and promoting primarily singing. The Corfu Music Conservatory is the second oldest active conservatory in Greece after that of Athens. It has two departments, music and drama, and a number of Schools, such as: the School of Higher Theoretical and Historical Classes, with vocal, harmony and band direction and organisation departments; Wind Instruments School; String Instruments School; Departments of Music for Pre-School Children; Byzantine and Ecclesiastical Music; and a School of Monody in collaboration with the Corfu Municipal Choir. It has also founded a School of Music Information, a department of which studies the use of computers in music, a department of modern and jazz music and a School of Greek Folk Music.

Easter

The *Epitaphios*

The town's three oldest philharmonic orchestras accompany the *epitaphios* bier along the length of its route, each always playing a specific piece: the red orchestra is the Old Philharmonic, which plays the Adagio by Albinoni; the blue orchestra is the Mantzaros Orchestra, which plays the Marcia Funebre by Giuseppe Verdi; and the Kapodistrias Philharmonic plays the Elegia Funebre, the Sventura by Mariani and Chopin's Funeral March. Purple lanterns are placed at the Liston arches on this day, increasing the atmosphere of grief. The first *epitaphios* biers to emerge are those of Panagia Spiliotissa from the New Fortress and that of Pantokrator at Kabielo at two o' clock in the afternoon, followed by the remaining churches until ten o' clock at night, when the *epitaphios* of the metropolitan church at Spilia comes out.

Breaking the pitchers and decorating the houses in the town with red textiles create a special sight at Easter.

Easter is celebrated with much splendour on the island and provides a wonderful experience for visitors. During this great celebration, the Orthodox and Catholic peoples on the island coexist harmoniously. The festival has strong influences from the Venetians and the tradition of idolatry. The church services are performed to the accompaniment of the philharmonic bands and polyphonic ecclesiastical music that came from Crete in the 17th century.

The Municipal Choir gives a concert of ecclesiastical music at the Municipal Theatre on **Holy Wednesday**. This annual performance was established in 1989, with the aim of experiencing the Divine Drama through western and eastern ecclesiastical music. On **Maundy Thursday** before the reading of the Twelve Gospels in the Catholic cathedral in Town Hall Square, they light twelve candles which are then extinguished one-by-one as each Gospel is read. On **Good Friday** the processions with the bier of Christ (*epitaphios*) start early in the afternoon, becoming more and more numerous until they almost overlap each other in the historical centre. The *epitaphioi* are followed by the philharmonic bands, choirs and crowds of faithful holding candles in their hands. From six o' clock in the morning on **Holy Saturday** at Panagia ton Xenon the custom of re-enacting the earthquake that took place after the Resurrection, as described in the Bible, is held. Later, at 9 am, the service of Saint Spyridon, established in 1550, is held. On the morning of Holy Saturday, during the time of the so-called "First" Resurrection there is a very special and peculiar noise that accompanies the ringing of the bells. It comes from the smashing of the clay pitchers (**bottides**), which the Corfiots throw from their balconies. This custom is closely connected to the remembrance of the joy of the Virgin Mary and Mary Magdalene who, according to tradition, were the first to see the open tomb of the resurrected Christ. According to another medieval tradition, the deafening sound made by the crashing of the pitchers wards off evil. Keeping a piece of the broken *bottides* in the house is believed to bring good luck. The custom of the *mastella* has been revived at Pinia, the town's old commercial centre. A half-barrel is decorated with myrtle and ribbons and passersby are invited to drop coins in for good luck. As soon as the first bell of the Resurrection rings out, someone dives in to collect the cash.

On the **evening of the Resurrection** itself the Metropolitan of Corfu and other officials ascend the platform that is erected on Spianada Square and at precisely the stoke of midnight, signalling Easter day and the proclamation "Christ Has Risen" ("Christos Anesti") they speak a few words of joy about the event and the fireworks are set off, while thousands of candles are lighted in the hands of the faithful gathered there. This is the only part of the town where the Resurrection of Christ

Impressive Resurrection fireworks at Spianada.

Above: The litany of St. Spyridonas, the patron saint of the island, entering Spianada (Copperplate, 1821).

is celebrated at midnight on Holy Saturday and that is why so many people gather there from all parts of the island. In some villages of Corfu they even have the custom of closing the church doors with the last 'Christ has risen', whilst the priest walks around it three times chanting. He then kicks in the central door and enters with the chant, 'Enter, enter, for the grace of God'. The other churches in the town as well as those in some of the villages celebrate the resurrection at sunrise Easter Day. After the proclamation "Christ is Risen" Spianada is transformed into a stage of dancing and high spirits as the resurrection ceremony gets into full swing. Easter Week is here called 'enia' or 'nia' (= nea, new) and its days are correspondingly called Enia Tuesday, Enia Wednesday, etc. The week is of great significance for worshippers and there are many events. On Easter Monday ('Nia Deftera') there are church services throughout almost the whole of the Prefecture of Corfu. Early in the morning, after the service, each church gets out its flabellum, hexapterygon and Cross.

The saints of Corfu and Paxoi

A number of saints chose to grace Corfu and Paxoi with their presence. Borderlanders, guardians of the borders between east and west, Orthodoxy and Catholicism.
Saints who are honoured by both churches, which today live side-by-side in peace.
Saint Spyridon, great patron and protector of Corfu (see page 92).
Saint Theodora the Augusta. Saint Theodora was born in Asia Minor in AD 815. In 830 she married the emperor Theophilus who, after his death in 842, made her empress (Augusta) of the Byzantine Empire as regent to his young son Michael. On a decision of the Holy Synod, on 11 February 842, a Sunday during Lent, they gathered in the church of Hagia Sophia and, with empress Theodora at their head, performed the service of the Holy Icons. The Greek Orthodox Church honours and celebrates this event on the first Sunday of Lent, which has been named the Feast of Orthodoxy. Saint Theodora died on 11 February 867. On 11 February and on the Feast of Orthodoxy there is a procession with her holy relics in her honour.
Saint Gaius, patron and protector of Paxoi. Saint Gaius was one of the seventy wise men who translated the Bible. Tradition holds that the saint fell ill whilst travelling to Rome and stopped at the port of Paxoi, where he died and was buried with honours. The church dedicated to his memory was built over the saint's tomb. On 29 June there is a service with the procession of his Holy Icon on Paxoi.

The Corfiots are a deeply religious people and this feeling is mainly focused on the worship of Ayios Spyridonas ("the Saint" as he is fondly known) who is considered to be the island's patron saint. The residents have very special and one could say, absolutely personal relations with him. His assistance is being constantly sought, whether the occasion be happy or sad. The intense religious sentiment is also evident in the many local fairs and feast-days. The most important, and the most spectacular, are those connected to the patron saint, Ayios Spyridonas, and which take place four times a year to the accompaniment of bands from all over the island.

1. Palm Sunday (at 11:00 am): On the anniversary of the rescue of Corfu from the plague in 1629. The religious procession begins from the church of the same name at eleven o' clock in the morning and follows the line where the town walls used to run along, from where the saint expelled the 'death'. This service has been held continuously since 1630, and today the island's eighteen philharmonic orchestras take part. In the evening there is a concert by the Mantzaros Philharmonic Society in the Municipal Theatre.

2. Holy Saturday (at 9:00 am.): These is the oldest litany of all and were established in the 16th century. Corfiots believe that the Saint have intervened to save the island from starvation by diverting into the harbour a number of grain ships which were actually destined elsewhere.

3. August 11 (at 11:00 am): which is celebrated in memory of the lifting of the Turkish siege of the town where tradition tells us that St. Spyridonas, in the guise of a monk and heading a band of angels, drove out the enemies holding the cross in one hand and a burning taper in the other.

4. The first Sunday in November (at 11:00 am): This service is held in remembrance of the island's salvation from a deadly attack of cholera which was acommplished once more with the intervention of Ayios Spyridonas. It was established in 1673 at the instigation of the Venetian government.

Church services

Above:
Moment from the service of Agios Spyridon, the island's patron saint.

The Theatre on Corfu

The characteristic Corfiot love of opera grew thanks to Venetian rule. Theatrical works have been performed in houses and squares since the early 16th century. With the creation of the San Giacomo Theater (the present Town Hall) in 1720 the musical and theatrical tradition of the island was firmly established.

Theatre of San Giacomo: in 1663 work started on the building of a portico in the centre of the town so as to provide a place for the local nobles to meet. In 1720 it was converted into a theatre and named the Theatre of San Giacomo. The building is in Renaissance style, built from carved Sinion stone, and its exterior is richly decorated with apses and baroque sculpture. At first it put on only Italian-language comedies and drama, with operas starting to be staged from the mid-18th century. Many operas had their Greek premieres here, whilst in 1833 the first performance in Greek lands featuring female actors was staged here (nine years before the appearance of women on the Athenian stage). In 1903 the Theatre of San Giacomo was converted into the Town Hall.

The beautiful Corfu Municipal Theatre: with 1000 seats and excellent acoustics, Corfu Municipal Theatre is considered to be one of the finest theatres in Europe. The first performance was given here in 1902 and in the following years the theatre experienced many moments of glory. It was destroyed by the Germans on 13 September 1943.

The new Municipal Theatre: the new Municipal Theatre was built in 1980, designed by Perikles Sakellarios a modernist architect of Corfiot descent. The theatre has a stage with a depth of seventeen metres and is fully equipped with seats for 850, a foyer, bar, and separate lecture and concert hall. Since July 1981 it has hosted thousands of productions and all types of events.

Corfu Municipal Regional Theatre (DIPETHE): in September 1983 the then Minister of Culture, Melina Merkouri, announced the creation of Municipal Regional Theatres. In 1997 Corfu was also incorporated into the network. These productions, eight of which have toured 62 different towns in Greece and Italy, have been seen by over 142,000 spectators. Each year the Regional Municipal Theatre also holds a cycle of events under the general title of 'May at the Phoinikas Theatre', where various arts companies (theatre, music, dance, etc) from the rest of Greece can perform their work.

Old photograph of the Theatre of San Giacomo.

info

Corfu Municipal Regional Theatre (DIPETHE)
68 G. Theotokis Street
49100 Corfu.
Tel. 26610 40156, 26610 40136

Scene from the Corfu theatre.

The Corfiots love of music can be witnessed at the festivals and fetes. This music can be heard here and there throughout the countryside during festivals. Songs sung to the accompianment of violins and guitars in the strong Ionian dialect have many elements that show the depth of their Italian roots. The music is a combination of Greek and Byzantine elements with Venetian and British influences. Serenades, folksongs, religious hymns and lyric operas all coexist in the same sounds. The first Greek composers lived and worked in the free Ionian Islands during the 19th century, where they brought the awakening Greek nation into contact with the European spirit. The first art music movement was born here, the **Septinsular School**, and this was the only occasion when modern Greek music was incorporated into contemporary European musical activity. A motivating figure in the creation of modern Greek music was the composer **Nikolaos Halikiopoulos Mantzaros** (1795-1872), who set Solomos' *Hymn to Freedom* to music, the first two versus of which are the Greek national anthem. The Philharmonic Society of Corfu was founded by him in 1840, the first such Society in Greece. Other important composers were **Spyridon Xyndas** (a student of Mantzaros) and **Spyridon Samaras**. In 1840 Xyndas, in collaboration with other artistic, cultural and political figures of Corfu, founded the Philharmonic Society of Corfu, the first Philharmonic Orchestra in Greek lands and the first institution teaching music in the wider Greek world. Samaras, one of the founders of the Italian opera school, was also the composer of the Olympic Hymn (Athens 1896). Later, the Kaisaris brothers were the first to form a band in Greece.

Musical tradition

Nikolaos Mantzaros

Nikolaos Mantzaros, born on Corfu in 1795, was one of the most celebrated Greek composers of the 19th century. Mantzaros studied music, first on Corfu and from 1819 in Italy where he became closely associated with the circle around the Royal Conservatory of Naples and its director Niccolò Antonio Zingarelli. He is considered the founder of the so-called 'Septinsular school of music' and was made life-long artistic director of the Philharmonic Society of Corfu in 1840. His finest work is considered the musical setting for the 'Hymn to Freedom' by Dionysios Solomos, which in 1865 was made the Greek national anthem. Mantzaros was the composer of the one-act comic opera *Don Crepuscolo* (1815), the first surviving operatic work by a Greek composer, as well as of the *Aria Greca* of 1827, the first-known piece for voice and orchestra in the Greek language, as well as the first known Greek pieces for a string quartet (*Partimenti*, circa 1850) and much more.

Philharmonic Bands

The philharmonic bands of Corfu are known throughout the world. They were founded during the general enthusiasm for starting clubs and associations of the 19th century. The first, the Philharmonic Society of Corfu, was founded in 1840 and today the island has eighteen philharmonic bands. All are non-profit organisations which aim at spreading musical awareness and perform at celebratory events on and outside of Corfu. The most important are the:

Mantzaros Philharmonic Society: This was founded in 1890 and has been running continuously for 110 years. It has successfully participated in philharmonic festivals in Bulgaria (1982 and 1985), been honoured at the Vienna festival in 1996 and in 1987 was awarded by the Academy of Athens.

Philharmonic Society of Corfu: Known in Corfu as the Old Philharmonic, it was founded in 1840. This is where Nikolaos Halkiopoulos Mantzaros taught music. The band was the first to perform the Greek national anthem and the first to perform the Olympic Hymn (by the Corfiot composer Spyridon Samaras) at the first modern Olympic Games in Athens in 1896. Today the Philharmonic Society has an orchestra of 150 musicians, a band of 90 musicians and a jazz band with 40 musicians. The Philharmonic Society has performed in many cities in Greece and abroad.

Kapodistrias Philharmonic Union: Founded in 1980 this is one of the largest and most important cultural organisations in Corfu, which specialises in music teaching. Its mission is to preserve, improve and promote the island's culture both on and off Corfu. The core of the Philharmonic Band is comprised of 150 musicians. Each section has a different uniform although always in the Kapodistrias Philharmonic Union's colours of red and black. It gives at least six to seven concerts a year, with classical works and pieces from opera and operetta. In the winter period it performs at the podium on the Upper Square, and has also successfully participated in many international festivals.

info

Philharmonic Society of Corfu
10 Nikiphorou Theotoki Street
Tel.: 226610 39298, 38765
www.fek.gr
Mantzaros Philharmonic Society
33 Philharmonikis Street
Tel.: 226610 37004
www.femantzaros.gr
Kapodistrias Philharmonic Union
2 Nikiphorou Theotoki Street
Tel.: 226610 33990

The emblem of the Philharmonic Society of Corfu. The owl symbolises wisdom and the musical instruments the art of sound.

The band of the Old Philharmonic.

The absence of Turkish rule, which supposedly terrorised the whole Aegean, and the influence of Byzantine and Venetian civilisation meant that a culture developed on Corfu that was bound to tradition but was also enriched by western culture.

Writing and Literature

One of the first educational institutes to be founded on Corfu was the Accademia dei Assicurati in 1656. This was followed by the Academia dei Fertili and the Quos Phoebus Errantes Vocat, which produced many important figures in the arts and letters. An important moment in the island's cultural development came with the founding of the famous **Ionian Academy**, which opened in 1824 and was the first institute of higher education in what is now Greece. The so-called **Septinsular School**, one of the most important trends in modern Greek literature, lasted from the late 18th century to the mid 20th century. Its characteristic feature is an insistence on the perfection of form and Dionysios Solomos is considered to be its main representative. Around him gathered a large literary circle, the Corfu School, the main representatives of which were Iakovos Polylas, Gerasimos Markoras, Ioannis Kalosgouros, Nikos Kogevinas, Lorentzos Mavilis and Konstantinos Theotokis. The almost exclusive use of the demotic language and an obsessive patriotism were characteristic features of the poetry of this period.

In 1836 the Literary Club was founded, the oldest cultural institute in what is now modern Greece, which was later renamed the **Corfu Reading Society**. Its members included Dionysios Solomos, Lorentzos Mavilis, Nikolaos Mantzaros and Konstantinos Theotokis. The rare collections in its Library are priceless. Another important cultural institution is the **Society of Corfiot Studies**, founded in 1952 and housed in the Solomos Mu-

where Homer's Phaeaceans still live, and East and West link hands like lovers, and everywhere the cypress blooms with the olive tree, mingling a somber mode with the blue that ticks the Boundless.

Kostis Palamas, 'Patrides'' (1904, trans. Mary Gregory)

Amongst the personalities who have had an influence on the culture of Corfu were the historian **Andreas Marmoras** (1618-1684) who was the first to write the history of the island, **Konstantinos Theotokis** (1731-1800) who was the first to introduce the natural sciences to Greece and who also translated many plays of Shakespeare, **Nikolaos Delviniotis** (1770-1850) who became famous thanks to his translation of the *Odyssey* into Italian, and the philosopher **Petros Vrailis Armenis** who pushed for modern Greek to be made the official language of the Ionian Republic.

ΡΗΓΑΣ Ο ΦΕΡΑΙΟΣ

Issue 19 by Rigas Velestenlis, 23 November 1871.

Corfu Presses

In spring 1798, following actions taken by the learned Pari, the first printing press in Greek lands, which was named the National Press (Ethniko Typographio) or the Press of the Race (tou Genous Typographio), was set up in the expropriated monastery of San Francesco in Corfu. From this time until the end of the British period in 1864 the press published all sorts of government documents of the French democrats, as well as the main speeches given at the Patriotic Society (Patrioti Etaireia) political club, and the Greek revolutionary pamphlets *Thourios* (War Song) and *Patriotikos Ymnos* (Patriotic Hymn) by Rigas Velestenlis and *Hymn to Bonaparte* by Christos Perraivos. The state press was opened with a special regulation on 22 April 1803 and in addition to public proclamations and state regulations it also printed newspapers and periodicals.

Corfiot costumes on 19th-century postcards from the first graphic arts workshop opened on the island in 1873.

seum. Its goal is to promote the intellectual life of the island through various activities. The **Society of Corfiot Studies** today continues the island's intellectual traditions, along with the Ionian University and the Corfu Reading Society. Today this intellectual tradition is carried on by the Association for Corfiot Studies of the Ionian University and the Reading Society.

Arts (Painting and Sculpture)

The art of Corfu has been influenced by the various conquerors and many artists who came to the island, bringing their knowledge and skills with them. The arts started to flourish on the island in the 16th century, with the arrival of many painters of the Cretan School. Even today on the island, in many churches and in the Byzantine Museum, there are icons by M. Damaskinos, Palladas, E. Lombardo, G. Kotzia and Georgios Kortezas, all of whom belonged to the Cretan School.

The most important names in painting in the next century are those of **Emmanuel Tzannes** and T. Poulakis. Emmanuel Tzannes was born in Crete but he lived in Corfu from 1646 to 1655 and many of his works can be found in the churches of Agios Iasonas and Sosipater, Agios Nikolaos Geronton, Panagia ton Xenon, Agios Georgios in the Old Fortress and the Byzantine Museum. **T. Poulakis** was from Crete and came to Corfu in the second half of the seventeenth century. His works can be seen in the Byzantine Museum, in a church at Kassiopi and in Platytera Monastery.

'May Day on Corfu' by M. Pachis (Ionian School, 19th century), National Gallery-Alexandros Soutzos Museum, Athens.

The 17th century was marked by the Venetian influence and the end of the Orthodox tradition in religious icons. This era produced many important painters, the most distinguished amongst them being P. Doxaras, who is considered to be the founder of the Ionian School of painting. Doxaras also worked in oils and his largest pieces is the decoration of the roof of the church of Agios Spyridon.

Only a few are aware that in 1811, during French rule, the first Greek School of Fine Arts was opened in Corfu, an important School worthy of comparison to those in Europe. The School was founded by the leading Corfiot painter **Pavlos Prosalentis**, the first Greek to work in a neoclassical style. Emblematic artists of the 19th-century tradition were: sculptor **D. Vegias** (the first Greek to use the technique of engraving); the landscape painter **Pachis**, who founded a painting school; A. Giallinas, who specialised in watercolours; the portrait painter G. Samartzis, who painted in a style reminiscent of French impressionism; and the painter and sculptor M. Zavitzianos, famous for his lithographs.

Church architecture

The religious heritage of the island is a rich one. Byzantine tradition and Western technique created a unique amalgam, both in an architectural and aesthetic sense. Most of the churches on Corfu were built between 1550-1750 and have many characteristics in common. The dominant style that one finds is that of the single-aisled wooden roofed basilica and more rarely the tripled-aisled basilica. An exception is the Byzantine church of Sts. Jason and Sosipatros, from the 12th century.

Panagiotis Doxaras: *The Holy Family.*

The western architectural features that one can see reflect the Venetians' prohibition of the erection of Byzantine churches. Characteristic of this are the tower-like belfries and the arrangement, usually without many variations, of the sanctuary, the main church and the women's loft. One of the peculiar features of the Ionian Island churches are the "ouranies", the various ceilings in the main church which have paintings in gilt and rather baroque frames.

The ceiling of the church of Agios Spyridon with scenes from the life of the saint and the four evangelists, by Panagiotis Doxaras.

Folk art

Corfu has also developed an great tradition of folk art. Weaving, embroidery and rugs are lavish in design and wonderfully subtle in their color combinations. Wicker work, other articles done in wood (furniture, chests, iconostases) and other small objects made of olive wood abound. There are many articles made of silver and jewellery with a broad range of decorative representations which have obviously been influenced by both Byzantine and Venetian art..

House architecture

Nearly all the villages contain large and beautiful mansions. Today most of them are locked and shuttered. Their owners, the descendants of the original estate owners, now live permanently in the town of Corfu. One can still see their coats-of-arms in the libraries of the palaces. Many of these are Venetian in origin and their families were listed in the Libro d'Oro of the Serene Republic of Venice.

The oldest houses that have still survived in the countryside are one or at the most two storey structures made of stone with a wooden roof. To reach the second floor one usually has to pass through the ground floor. They have very simple lay-outs and clearly a survival of the Byzantine house that is found throughout Greece.

Later when the threat presented by marauders and pirates passed, the exteriors of the houses were embellished with a number of elements which today give them their special traditional character. There is external access to the second floor via a stone staircase which ends at a covered landing, the "bontzo" through which one enters the ground floor through the "volto". This special kind of veranda gets wider as on goes further inside and at one time supported on brick columns the "xychyti" the covered area which was usually an extension of one side of the roof. Similar areas were also found on the ground floor supported on heavy columns and throughout Greece they have created a somewhat private and somewhat public space for relaxation and conversation.

This "xychyti" is a basic element of an architecture of temperate climate favoured by sun. It is the "liakoto" or "iliakos" (the "sun - room") of the ancients which when properly oriented allows the winter sun to enter the house while in the summer when the sun is high it makes for a shady facade and a feeling of coolness.

Characteristic lane in the old town.

The Megaron Kapodistrias, the building of the old Prefecture on Kapodistrias Street, was built during the British period as the residence of the family of the first Governor of Greece, Ioannis Kapodistrias. It was designed by Ioannis Chronis (a Corfiot architect who designed many public buildings in the town, including the Ionian Parliament and the Ionian Bank), in 1832 and is an exceptional example of neoclassical architecture. Many sections are carved from pink Sinion stone, whilst carved white marble has been used in the ground floor and mezzanine. The ceilings have been decorated with wonderful paintings. The external facade of the building is adorned with elegant pilasters in the Corinthian order. Today it houses the offices of the Ionian University.

Ricci Mansion

(15 Moustoxydi Street, Platy Kantouni)

The Ricci Mansion is one of the most interesting Venetian mansions in Corfu town, dating most probably to the 17th century. It initially had two floors. It has a portico on the ground floor with an elegant arcade, the peaks of the arches of which are decorated with sculpted male and female heads reminiscent of the decoration on the Loggia. A comfortable balcony is set above the portico, from where, during the Venetian period, the town leaders would watch the jousts that were held in the street below during Carnival.

Corfu town. Aerial photograph.
The Old Fortress can be seen in the background.

Museums and Libraries

Introduction

In an area so full of monuments and places of historical interest, there, of course, have to be an equivalent number of museums and other sites where one can find collections that illustrate the island's history. The Corfiots, however, with the love they nurture in their souls for culture, are not satisfied with simply zealously protecting what was handed down to them by their ancestors from the prehistoric up to the present, but have forged ahead and created museums and cultural centers which contain objects that are not only rare in Greece but anywhere in Europe; in fact anywhere in the world. This Archaeological Museum which presents to the visitor the most important finds from ancient Corfu, the Byzantine Museum which tells the story of the rise, fall and continuity of the Byzantine Empire, are all part of a single context with the Currency Museum, a totally unique place, the Dionysios Solomos Museum, in honor of Greece's national poet, the Municipal Gal-lery and the Reading Society with its highly important Ionian Library. Finally, there is the real gem of Corfu, the truly significant Museum of Asian Art, with exhibits that were collected by eminent Greek diplomats, from throughout the East; this completes the cultural cornucopia of Corfu making it a place that has a great deal to offer every visitor in terms of culture and not just as a superb tourist site.

Opposite page: The enormous stone pediment from the Doric temple to Artemis, its central motif being the monstrous Gorgon.

Below: Room in the Museum of Asian Art.

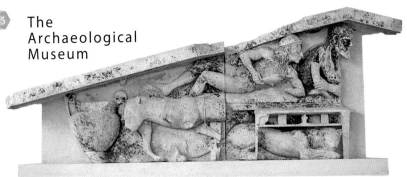

Section of a late Archaic pediment (circa 500 B.C.) from the area of Figareto on Cape Kanoni. It was found right next to Chalkiopoulos salt lake which was the Yllaikos harbor of ancient Corfu. The approximate length of the pediment is 11 meters and shows a scene from a Dionysian symposium.

info

1 Vraila Armeni Street
Tel. 26610 30680.
Opening hours:
Summer months: 08.00 - 19:30
Daily except Mondays.
Winter months: 08.30 - 15:00
Daily except Mondays.

The Archaeological Museum of Corfu is near Garitsa, the avenue along the waterfront. This museum contains primarily the sculptural remains from the temple of Artemis which the experts have concluded was built during the period 590-580 B.C, in the area of Kanoni which was the site of ancient Corfu. Enormous and unique is the stone frieze from the temple of Artemis. Enormous because it is 17 meters wide and more than three meters high! Unique because it is the largest group of Archaic monumental sculpture (beginning of the 6th century B.C.). The main subject matter is the monstrous Gorgon who is framed by her two children, Pegasus and Chryssaorus and two lions. Both sides of the frieze have retained parts of depictions of the Battle of the Titans.

The other exhibits are:
- Bits and pieces from the earliest Neolithic period (6th millennium B.C.), flint stones, vases and tools from the Bronze Age.
- Corinthian vases as well as Corfiot copies that come from the tombs at Garitsa (7th and 6th century B.C.).

- Coins among which there is the silver drachma with the depiction of a cow which was minted during the time Corfu regained its independence from Corinth.
- Parts of the roof of the Temple of Roda (5th century).
- Lead plaques (6th and 5th century) with inscriptions which declare that certain debts are owed.
- Small bronze statues from classical ancient art.
- An Attican black-figured wash-basin from the 6th century with depictions of lions.
- Pieces from the great temple to Hera. What are of worth are the acrokerama in the shape of a lion's head (end of the 7th century).
- Small objects made of clay, bronze and ivory.
- Small clay statues of Artemis from the small temple dedicated to her at Kanoni.
- Various works (mainly in terracotta) which were done between the fourth century B.C. and Roman times.
- There is also another very important work, an Archaic lion which was made toward the end of the 7th century by a gifted Corinthian sculptor. It was found right next to the monument of Menecrates.

Archaic lion from the 7th century which was found near the tomb of Menecrates.

Bronze statuette of a reveller holding a rhyton, found at Mon Repos.

Marble head of the Athenian comic poet Menander, from the 4th century BC, and the historian Thucydides (Roman copy of 300 BC).

Museum of Asiatic Art

info

Palace of St Michael
and St George.
Tel. 26610 30443.
Opening hours:
Summer months: 08.00 - 19:30
Daily except Mondays.
Winter months: 08.30 - 15:00
Daily except Mondays.

The Museum of Asian Art, founded in 1927, is the only one of its kind in Greece and consists of the large collection (approximately 10,000 objects) of the Corfiot diplomat Grigorios Manos and then further supplemented by the collection of the former ambassador N. Chatzivasileiou (around 200 objects) and two smaller collections belonging to the diplomats I. Siniosoglou and P. Alamanachos respectively. Several of the exhibits in the museum are considered to be of exceptional value, even on an international scale. The works in the museum of particular interest are the following:

· Artistic ornaments made of bronze (mainly brass) from the time that China entered the historical period (Shang period, 1500-1027 B.C.).

· Clay objects from the Chinese Chou period (1027-221 B.C.).

· Small statue and an interesting cast of a house of Chinese art from the Han Dynasty (221 B.C. until 220 A.D.).

· Bronze statue of Buddha from the Sung dynasty (960-1297 A.D.)

· Bronze pottery, small statues of porcelain and sandstone, porcelain vases done in the world-famous blue color and various small ivory objects made during the Ming dynasty (a period when the arts truly flourished in China under the great flowering of Confucianism, 1368-1644).

Japanese mask from the No Theater.

· Various small objects made of semi-precious stones and ivory and porcelain items decorated with coats-of arms, naked female figures and so on and so forth, bottles made of porcelain, glass and semi-precious stones, furniture, textiles and fabrics from the Ch'ing dynasty (1644-1912).

· Small statues and other objects d'art from the oldest Japanese period (Yagoi, 250 B.C. until 250 A.D.).

· Statuettes from the Kamakura Japanese period (1192-1338). Among them is a very distinctive, and angry temple guard, made of wood.

Demon with his companion (Tantra).

· Weapons and pieces of Samurai armor from the period between the 16th and the 18th century. Masks from the No Theater belonging to the period of Muromachi or Ashigkaga (1338-1578) and a picture of the popular Kabuki Theater.

· A screen with a depiction of mounted Samurai.

· Various small objects from the period between the 17th and the 19th century.

· Ceramics, fans, ink-stand, stamped pictures, lacquered wooden objects and various samples of calligraphy.

· Indian wood carvings with erotic depictions full of religious symbolism, painted Korean screens, sculptural works from Siam, bronze statues from Tibet, sculpture from Gandara (the "Greek-Buddhist" School of northwestern India) dating from the 1st to the 5th century AD, with clear Hellenistic influences, the legacy of Alexander the Great's presence in the region and much else.

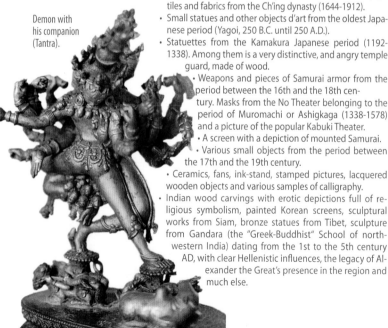

Porcelain vases with the characteristic blue colour.

Bronze statue of Buddha, Sung Dynasty.

An 11th century wood-carving from India.

A Japanese woodcut from the Edo period (18th-19th century).

Solomos Museum and Society of Corfiot Studies

info

1 Arseniou Street, Mouragia.
Tel. 26610 30674..
Opening hours:
Tuesday-Sunday: 08.30-15.00.
Closed Mondays.

It is widely known that the Greek national poet Dionysius Solomos lived most of his life (1798-1857) and until his death on Corfu, where he wrote the largest and finest part of his literary output, including the 'Free Besieged'. The Centre for Solomos Studies was established in the poet's former house by the Society of Corfiot Studies, and it also functions as the Solomos Museum. The exhibition includes furniture and personal effects, photographs and historical documents from the life and work of the great poet. There is also a fine Solomos Library, which is continuously being added to and the collections of which include all the old editions of the 'Hymn to Freedom', otherwise known as the Greek national anthem. You can also see a series of portraits of the poet and other members of the so-called Solomos School. The building also houses the **Society of Corfiot Studies**, founded in 1952 by the distinguished historian and journalist of the island, Kostas Dafnis. The Society's goals are to promote the cultural and artistic life of Corfu, the documentation and study of local history, economy and folklore, and the foundation and maintenance of public reading rooms and libraries in Corfu town and the countryside.

Banknote Museum

info

Iroon Kypriakou Agona Square
(Agios Spyridon Square).
Tel. 26610 41552.
Opening hours:
Summer months: 10:00 - 14:00
Daily except Saturday
and Sunday.
In the winter months the Banknote Museum is open only for visitor groups (schools, universities and tourist groups) on prior arrangement:
tel. 26610 80342.

The Banknote Museum was founded by the Ionian Bank in 1981 and is the only one of its kind in Greece and one of the few in the world with an exhibition of banknotes, coins, stamps, banking documents, printing casts and models. The exhibition includes a display that follows all the stages in the production of banknotes: from the initial design and production of the paper to the destruction of old banknotes in special kilns.

In one Room of the Museum you can see a display of the processes involved in the production of banknotes. Of particular interest is the section on the creation of the watermark, which is integrated into the banknote. In this same area there is a small workshop where you can see the designs being engraved onto metal plates.

The Kapodistrias Museum and Centre of Kapodistrian Studies was founded in 1981, having been donated by Maria Desylla-Kapodistria. The house and property are located in Koukouritsa in the village of Evropouloi and were part of the estate of the Governor's family during his lifetime. The exhibits on display here include personal items of Ioannis Kapodistrias and period furniture.

Kapodistrias Museum

info

Centre of Kapodistrian Studies,
Evropouloi.
Tel. 6610 39528 & 26610 32440.
Opening hours:
Closed Mondays.
Tuesday-Sunday: 10.30-14.00.

The Museum of Ceramic Arts includes a large number of the surviving examples of Corfiot ceramics, an art form that was thriving in the past. Corfiot production started in the mid-16th century and reached its peak in the late 18th and early 19th century, providing Corfu's first industrial income. Although the ceramic work of Corfu never reached an especially high level of artistic quality they are, nonetheless, fine pieces of folk art distinguished for their elegant lines, the variety of shapes and their simple painted decoration

Museum of Ceramic Arts

info

British Barracks
New Fortress.
Tel. 26610 27370.

The Serbian Museum exhibits material on the tragedy of

the Serbian soldiers during the First World War. Photographs from their three-year stay in Corfu comprise the largest part of the exhibition, alongside the uniforms, weapons and equipment of the Serbian soldiers and officers. There are also Serbian regimental flags, ecclesiastical vestments and various other items belonging to Serbian priests, the surgical tools of Serbian doctors from Vido island in 1916, and medals and other decorations of the Kingdom of Serbia.

Serbian Museum
The Serbs in Corfu, 1916-1918

info

19 Moustoxydi Street,
Spianada, on the Kapodistrias Street side,
Tel. 26610 33960.

Corfu Byzantine Collection

info

Central gate of the Old Fortress
Tel. 26610 48310, 48120.
Opening hours:
1 July to 31 October:
Daily: 08.30 - 19.30
Closed Mondays.

Agios Georgios (late 15th-16th century, Cretan influence). This type of icon painting, with the small slave who was liberated, developed in Crete in the 15th century and was widely diffused until the 17th century.

The Corfu Byzantine Collection is a rich collection of approximately 100 icons that cover a period of three centuries, from the 14th to the 17th century, with portraits of saints and biblical scenes. Around forty of the exhibits in the Collection are part of the Byzantine collection of the Museum of Asian Art. It contains Early Christian architectural sculpture and sections of mosaic floors of churches from the Old Town (see p. 74), fragments of Byzantine wall paintings from the church of Ayios Nikolaos (St. Nicolas) of Kato Korakiana (11th, 13th and 18th century and a very interesting collection of icons from the period between the 16th and the 18th century. These are works of art that have been transferred there from various churches on the island and were made by the likes of Michael Damaskinos, Emmanuel Lombardos, The. Poulakis, Ioannis Tsinos and E. Tzane Bounialis. The Collection includes the mosaics from the basilica at Palaiopoliw, uncovered during the excavations that took place from 1930 to 1959. Other fine exhibits in the Collection include sculptures and marble and limestone architectural pieces of the 11th, 12th and 13th centuries from various Byzantine monuments of Corfu.

Byzantine Museum of Antivouniotissa

info

Church of the Panagia Antivouniotissa,
Arseniou Street,
Kabielo, Old Town.
Tel. 26610-38313.
www.antivouniotissamuseum.gr
Opening hours:
Tuesday to Sunday: 08:30 - 15:00
Closed Mondays.
The Museum is closed on 25/12, 1/1, 25/3, 1/5, Easter Sunday and May Day.

The Byzantine Museum was founded with a donation in 1979. The Museum's collections include Byzantine and post-Byzantine works by Emmanuel Tzannes, M. Avramis, N. Tzafouris, Michail Damaskinos, Stephanos Tzankarolas, I. Palladas, Emmanuel Lambardou and others.

The Museum's finest pieces include:

- The icon of the Theotokou Hodegetria, where the Panagia (Virgin Mary) is represented holding the infant Christ. In the upper corners are the heads of the archangels Gabriel and Michael. The icon is dated to the late 15th century and is a work of Emmanuel Lambardou.
- The icon of saints Sergius, Bacchus and Justine, with the saints trampling upon a three-bodied dragon. This is a work of Michail Damaskinos and refers to the victory of the European powers at the Battle of Lepanto in 1571.
- The icon of Saint Dimitrios showing the saint on horseback, in front of Thessaloniki. A work of the late 16th century or early decades of the 17th century.
- The icon of Saint Cyril of Alexandria, with the saint shown in full-figure, frontally and wearing rich vestments. Emmanuel Tzannes, 1654.
- The icon titled 'Touch me not', showing the meeting between Christ and Mary Magdalene after the Resurrection. Emmanuel Tzannes, 1657.
- In the main church are exhibited other equally important icons, such as the Christ Pantokrator by Emmanuel Lombardo and Saint Alexios by Stephanos Tzankarolas.

Three Archangels in the north narthex. Georgios Kortezas, first half 17th century, egg tempura on wood.

The Reading Society

info

120 Kapodistriou Street
Tel. 26610 39528.
www.anagnostikicorfu.com
Opening hours:
Daily except Sundays
9.00–14.00.

It is the oldest intellectual foundation in modern Greece, being founded in 1836 and its members have always been eminent Ionian Islander and foreigners from the the world of the intellect and the arts. Among them were Kapodistrias, Kalvos, Solomos, Mantzaros, Markoras, Theotokis and Lorentzios Mavilis.

It has a well-stocked library of general interest, a collection of paintings and engravings, old maps, publications, newspapers and photographs. But what really sets it apart are the nearly 10,00 volumes of Ionian island bibliography.

It works in collaboration with Greek and foreign universities and scientific foundations. Since 1978 it has been a member of "Europe Nostra" which is concerned with the protection and the promulgation of our architectural, historical and natural heritage.

Recently the activities of the Society have been expanded. It plays host to painting, engraving and photographic exhibitions. It also holds scientific conferences, lectures and seminars and in addition public and private musical recitals.

The Society publishes a Bulletin containing research work -primarily into Corfiot subjects- and has also issued a deluxe collection of religious icons from the island. Among its other publications is a 5000 word glossary of Corfiot dialect.

Interior and exterior views of the Corfu Reading Society.

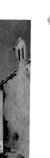

'The Murder of Kapodistrias' by Haralambos Pachis.

Municipal Gallery

The Municipal Gallery opened in 1978. Most of the works in the collection came from donations by various collectors and artists of the 19th and 20th centuries. The exhibits in the Gallery include some of the finest works by Ionian painters of the 19th century. The Municipal Gallery contains works by primarily Corfiot artists, including Haralambos Pachis, founder of the Corfu school of art, the water-painter Angelos Giallinas, Spyridon Skarvelis, who decorated the Achilleion, Spyros Prosalentis, the icon painter Michail Damaskinos, Pavlos Prosalentis the younger, Vikentios Bokacciambis, Georgios Samartzis, and the painters and engravers Lykourgos Kogevinas and Nikolaos Ventouras. In addition to the permanent exhibition, the Museum also holds temporary exhibitions, lectures, presentations, art history classes, concerts and educational programmes for children.

Some of the most important works in the Gallery are:

- Michail Damaskinos, 'The Beheading of John the Baptist' and 'The stoning of St Stephen'.
- Haralambos Pachis, 'The Murder of Kapodistrias'.
- Angelos Giallinas, 'Markas'.
- Georgios Samartzis, 'Night on Corfu'.
- Nikolaos Ventouras, 'The house of Giallinas' and 'Vianello's Lane'.
- Aglaia Pappa, 'Self-portrait'.
- Spyros Prosalentis, 'Warrior of 1821'.

info

Palace of St Michael and St George.
1 Akadimias Street.
Tel. 26610 39553.
Opening hours:
Closed Mondays.
Tuesday-Sunday: 08.30-15.00
Temporary exhibitions are open in the mornings and evenings (10.00-13.00 and 18.00-21.00), whilst the permanent exhibitions are open continuously (9.30-15.00).

Mon Repos Palaiopoli Museum

info

Mon Repos
Tel. 26610 41369.
Opening hours:
Tuesday-Sunday: 08.30-15.00.
Closed Mondays.

Within the gardens of Palaiopoli you will find the palace of Mon Repos, which was first built in 1826 by the British high commissioner Frederick Adam and which subsequently passed into the possession of the Greek royal family. The exhibition inside the Mon Repos Museum seeks to inform the visitor on the uses of the building and the history of the site from antiquity until the present day. The exhibition on the ground floor includes artefacts relating to the life and use of the building (such as documents, portraits and furniture), as well as the broader region in the 19th century (such as the collection of plant paintings). On the first floor are exhibited finds from the excavations in the ancient town which are related to trade, public and private life and the worship of the ancient Corfiots.

General State Archives of the Prefecture of Corfu

info

British Barracks,
Old Fortress.
Tel. 26610 38193.

The Corfu Archives are now housed in the buildings of the former British Barracks in the Old Fortress, covering the period 1320 from 1537 sporadically and that from 1538 to today more completely. It preserves the collective memory of over six centuries and is one of the largest archives in Greece (with approximately 8,500 metres of stored material) and with the richest collection of historical documents, having operated continuously since 1443. It has valuable collections of parchment documents, architectural designs and maps and is run according to the latest European standards.

Astronomical Society

info

2nd Floor,
Municipal Theatre.
Tel. 26610 38278.
Opening hours:
Mondays and Thursdays
17.00-21.00.

The Corfu Observatory was built in 1924 by the Frenchman Felix Chemla Lamech. Three years later, in 1927, the Astronomical Society of Greece was founded, the only one in Greece, and also in 1927 it began to publish its newsletter 'Ourania' in Greek and French and sometimes in German and English. The Astronomical Society's important activities made Corfu known throughout the world in this field, for which reason it was honoured by the Academy of Athens in 1932. The Astronomical Society is active in many areas: it organises observations of the night sky, screens films, holds events and lectures by distinguished Greek scientists and participates in Greek and European conferences.

The Museum was founded in September 2010 and is the only one of its kind in Greece. It attempts to trace the history of the Philharmonic over the past two centuries of continuous activity, within exhibits of important artefacts such as instruments, portraits, class registers, photographs, musical scores and sound recordings. The Museum is named after and thus honours the great Corfiot musician and the Philharmonic's first artistic director, Nikolaos Halkiopoulos Mantzaros.

Nikolaos Mantzaros Museum of Music

info

10 Nikiphorou Theotoki Street.
On the 1st floor of the
Philharmonic Society building.
Tel. 22610 39289.
http://museum.fek.gr
Opening hours:
Monday to Friday
09.30-13.30.

The Public Library of Corfu is the oldest in Greece. Jacob Francis Xaverio Canal, deputy Archbishop of the Latin Diocese of Corfu for many years, donated the first nucleus of the Public Library. He died in 1758, having let to the Corfu Community the excellent and sizeable library that he kept in the convent of Santa Giustina in Garitsa. During the Septinsular Republic the Library was enriched through purchases and donations, reaching 7,000 volumes. The Library Stamp was made, with the emblem of the Corfiot trireme and around it the words *Bibliotheca Publica Corcyrese*. The Library organises book exhibitions and conferences and hoses around 75,000 publications. The Library plays an important role in spreading the value of book-reading, especially amongst young people.

Public Library

info

British Barracks,
Old Fortress.
Tel. 26610 38195.

The Ionian Society of Historical Studies was founded on Corfu in 1992, following an initiative by students, professors and graduates of the Department of History at the Ionian University. The Society publishes the academic periodical *Peri Istorias*, and its aim is to produce fertile historical dialogue on the sources of Septinsular history, the exploration of unknown aspects of modern Greek history (Second World War occupation, post-war period) as well as to promote young scholars and academics. The Society also organises one-day conferences and lectures on historical, literary, and general scholarly issues.

Ionian Society of Historical Studies

info

Department of History,
Ionian University,
72 Ioannou Theotoki Street.
www.ionio.gr

Corfu town

Introduction The image that one takes away of the town of Corfu has always been especially compelling down through all the various historical periods of its development. Fortified since ancient times, the town's castles still exist which were built by the ancient Corfiots, and the Byzantines but which have frequently been augmented by the town's other conquerors and with their impressive mass have come to form the town's crowning point. On the Balkan shores opposite one can still seem to hear the eternal clash of peoples and cultures, be it peaceful or violent, but always with a kind of savage beauty, a clash that has never ceased for long on those mountains across the way. But the town of Corfu itself with its merry and friendly inhabitants seems a world apart from those mountains.

Its streets may still carry the sounds of distant clashes but today they are ruled by high spirits, music and beauty. Approaching the town by ship, a moist and misty feeling of the sea creates an ethereal image of the town which makes it seem like a fleeting vision. Getting closer one sees the

info

Corfu Old Town, with the Old and New Fortress, is inscribed on UNESCO's list of world heritage sites as an outstanding architectural ensemble representing an important historical period.

dense mass of houses built amphitheatrically around the harbor. The town's old houses give one a quite unique aesthetic pleasure.

The town of Corfu can be divided into three sections: The **old town**, with its narrow alleys and the Old Castle, the **new town** with the commercial harbour and the shopping district. Finally its **hinterland** which includes the renowned Kanoni and the famous Pontikonisi, which will be described in the following chapter.

The Old Town developed in a very limited space, between two fortresses and surrounded by walls. The only answer to the increasing population was the building of multi-storeyed buildings, the one right next to the other, made of stone but with no concrete reinforcement, with tiled roofs and attics. Fortunately there were no earthquakes in Corfu like the rest of the Ionian islands (1953) so the Old Town has remained, in essence, intact. Corfu owes a good deal of its fame to this old town.

One can spend seemingly endless hours wandering through the narrow flagstoned lanes enjoying the sudden discovery of a small flagged square with a single palm tree in the middle amid the all the tall houses set side by side. Hidden courtyards and stone staircases, ornate balconies and elaborately framed windows with an occasional view of the sea peeking out between the houses.

OLD TOWN

The Old Town is comprised of the neighbourhoods of Kabielo, Mouragia, Spilia, the Jewish quarter, the district of Porta Riala, Porta Remounta, Kantelakoues (Cantelle d'Aqua, Street of Waters), the Piazza, Agios Spyridon Square, Pinia (cones), the district of Kofineta and Liston, and Spianada (the large square of Corfu).

Panoramic view of Corfu town.

Spianada
Liston

The tour of the town of Corfu starts off from Spianada the large open space lying between the town and the Old Fortress. The original reason that this space was left open was that the gunners from the fortress would have an open range of fire against any prospective invader. At the same time it was also useful for military parades.

Today the southern part has been transformed into a charming park, with a bandstand, statues and shady paths and the northern part is an up-to-date cricket pitch. Cricket and Ginger Beer are among the few customs left from the British occupation. But the French were, in actual fact, the first to think of planting trees on Spianada.

Despite the various origins of the buildings surrounding Spianada - Venetian, French, British and Greek - they have managed to become a harmonic unit which bathed in the soft light of Corfu are very pleasing to the eye.

Going towards Liston, on your right you will see the **monument commemorating the Union of the Ionian Islands with Greece**. Further down, having gone down a few steps, is the **Venetian spring**, which today has been converted into a fountain. Walking to the left we come to the popular **Pentofanaro**, where on Easter Saturday the First Resurrection is marked with the smashing of the *bottides* pitchers

The building on the west side of Spianada is one of the town's pride and joys. This is the vaulted gallery with cafes and restaurants known as the "**Liston**", built during the brief second period of the French occupation (1807-1814) based on the plans of the engineer Lesseps using the Parisian Rue Rivole as a model. The cafes in Liston are the center of social life in Corfu and the hustle and bustle go on throughout the year.

On the southernmost tip of Spianada there is a building, which in 1840 came to house the **Ionian Academy** (see page 24) and thus contributed to Corfu being the most important center for Greek art and culture.

The Maitland Monument is an elegant, simple, circular, Ionic monument built in honour of the second British Lord High Commissioner of the Ionian Islands, Sir Thomas Maitland (1816-1824), although he was also the most severe commissioner. It was built by the British army engineer G. Whitemore, who also designed the Palace of St Michael and St George, made of Maltese stone with sculptural decoration by the Corfiot sculptor Prosalentis. Opposite the Maitland Monument is Iroon Agoniston Polytechniou Square, with the sculpture of Dionysius Solomos.

Ionian Academy

The building was designed by the important Corfiot architect Ioannis Chronis, and it has an elegant neoclassical simplicity. The facade is symmetrically arranged with the entrance, on the raised ground floor, being emphasised by a double stairway. The next two floors have small balconies centrally arranged over the entrance to the building. It is used for cultural events (conferences, lectures, cinema screenings, and theatre, music and dance productions). Tel. 26610 87609.

The Venetian fountain at Spianada.

Enoseos Square with the small stage where the Resurrection service is held at Easter and concerts are given by the Philharmonic bands.

The cafes of Liston in the west square of Spianada.

The Palace of Sts. Michael and George

The entire northern side of Spianada is occupied by the Palace of the Sts. George and Michael. This superb neoclassical building with the Doric colonnade on the facade, made with special porous stone that was brought from Malta, fits in perfectly with the surrounding buildings. It was designed by Colonel George Whitmore in 1819 as the dwelling of the High Commissioner. The idea for the overall composition was derived from the large country houses that the English aristocrats had on their estates in the countryside. It is the only monument built in the Georgian style throughout the entire Mediterranean. It also housed the Ionian Senate and the offices of the Orders of Sts. Michael and George. During the years 1846-1913 it was used as a summer residence by the Greek royal family but was then abandoned.

The 18th-century Panagia Mandrakina near the Palace, dedicated to the Panagia (Virgin Mary) and Saint Panteleimon. The building has an elaborate symmetrical facade with a pedimental peak. The Tuscan Doric pillars on the facade and the four-sided tower-shaped belfry with an elaborate peak, renovated in 1860 by the architect Ioannis Chronis, are especially impressive.

Interior and exterior view from the Palace.

Recently it has been renovated and now houses the Museum for Asian Art (see chapter museums), the Historical Archives and the Ephor of Classical Antiquities. On the frieze of the palace there are allegorical reliefs of the seven Ionian islands and Corfu is represented as a ship. The impressive main reception hall on the ground floor is ornamented with two rows of Ionic columns and with scenes that have been reproduced from the *Odyssey*.

To the rear is a broad, grand staircase which half-way up divides and leads to the antechamber on the second floor, with its Corinthian columns.

Opposite the staircase are the three main halls of the palace: the main, round one, the ballroom, while to the left was the Throne Room and to the right the Banquet Hall. These are the places where the summit meeting of the European Union were held in 1994.

The Old Fortress is the easternmost point of the headland on which the town of Corfu is built. The entrance to the Old Fortress or Fortezza, in practically opposite the Liston. The fortifications are a marvel of military architecture and it is worthwhile paying the garrison a visit both to observe the architecture and to enjoy the view.

It is easy enough for one to understand why this spot was considered ideal during the building of a fortified town. It is easy to defend from the mainland and since it juts out into the sea it can be readily used as a point of control for marine traffic. On the north side of the acropolis a small, artificial lake was created while further north a natural bay was developed which was also used as a harbor.

The first fortification works were done by the Byzantines at the beginning of the 8th century and they appear to have consisted of a wall facing dry land and the first moat. There were few changes or additions until the 16th century when Venetians who controlled Corfu was threatened by the Turks, leading to the fortification of the entire town. During that period more bastions were built, the imposing western gate was constructed and the moat enlarged. To create a second defensive line another moat was dug within the external walls and there was a third line of defense around the two high points of land. The sides of these elevations were smoothed until the scaling of the bare rock would become practically impossible for invaders. The remnants of the defensive works that can still be seen today are by and large the fortifications built by the Venetians in the 16th century.

In front of the Fortress is a **statue of General Schulenberg**, the defender of Corfu against the Turks, an offering made by the grateful Venetians in 1715 (while he was still alive) which was originally inside the fortress.

After crossing the bridge over the first moat, the "Contra Fossa" where fishing boats and pleasure craft are now moored, you pass through the Fortress gate and then cross the second moat and enter the first interior courtyard. The plaque on the wall opposite you as you enter the courtyard commemorates the union of the Ionian Islands with Greece in 1864. From here a stairway leads through a long and curving tunnel which reaches the heart of the fortified area.

As we approach the end of the tunnel a path on the left leads us to the north battlements of the fortress, which are located above a small lake, Lake Mandraki, where yachts moor today. Mandraki is an artificial harbour where the Venetian fleet moored during war. Its square shape allowed it to be spacious and it is said that it could hold

The Old Fortress

The entrance is through Spianada, where two small obelisks form the outer gate to the Fortress. At their bottom, two Venetian bombards bear the date 1684 and, on their upper part, the coat-of-arms of Roberto Papafana, governor of Corfu from 1706-1709. Today's bridge, built by the British in 1819, has a length of sixty metres and a height of fifteen metres above the water. The fortress's original bridge was wooden and movable so that the fortress island could be cut off in times of need. The statue of General Schulenburg stands in front of the Old Fortress.

The statue of General Schulenburg stands before the old Fortress.

The island of Vido

The island of Vido is located at a distance of 1200 metres from the old port and is divided from the Old Fortress by a narrow sea channel. The name Vido is attributed to one of the former owners of the island, Guido Malipieri, whose name was corrupted from Guido to Vido. On this little island one can see the **Serbian mausoleum** set up by the Serbian government in memory of the Serbian soldiers who died on Corfu between 1914 in 1918 when they were forced to abandon Serbia, persecuted by Austrian troops. The historic **church of Agios Stephanos** is also here, repaired and renovated. Information: on the islet there is a restaurant, doctor's surgery, organised beach and footpaths for walking through the beautiful natural landscape.

Information: You can reach the islet by boat from the old port. Departure times from Corfu port: hourly from 9 am to 9 pm. Departure times from Vido: every half hour from 9.30 am to 9.30 pm. Campsite office and manager of Vido island: tel. 26610 44222.

'ten *katerga*' (galleys) of 500 tons and other smaller ships. The island in the background is called the island of Vido and nobody had thought to fortify it before the French came along.

The island in the background is called "**the island of Vido**" and before the French arrived no one had thought to fortify it. Its bastions and fortifications were destroyed by the British.

At the end of the tunnel the path leads to the abandoned barracks. At this point another path begins which ends at the other high point of the fortress, where clearly the original fortifications were located. The main charm of the Fortress is the superb view of the town it offers and the passage to the mainland opposite. Winter and spring the light outlines the snow-covered peaks of Epirus so clearly you would think that by stretching out your hand you could touch them.

What one should really see inside the fortress is the **side-chapel of Ayios Georgios** (St. George) which is a strange neoclassical structure the British built in 1840. It is located on the south side of the hill.

The Kontra Fosa moat, which cut the Old Fortress off from the town thus reinforcing its defences.

The church of Agios Georgios is one of the largest on Corfu. It was built in 1840 on designs of the British military architect Emmett so as to serve the religious needs of the British garrison. It has been built in the so-called Georgian order and is reminiscent of an ancient Doric temple. The church's original internal structure has been adapted as a result of the destruction it suffered during the Second World War. Some of the original icons still survive in the icon screen and these are attributed to the painter Emmanuel Tzannes (17th century). There are also more recent paintings inside the church. The Divine Liturgy is performed in this church only once a year now, on the feast day of Saint George, although archaeological exhibitions with religious art and musical and other events are held in here from time to time.

Aerial photograph of the Old Fortress.

From Spianada to the Old Harbor

A pleasant stroll takes you along the coast (the Mouragia area). You go past the palace on the north side of Spianada. From the courtyard which lies to the left of the building, after the **St. George Gate**, you can see the **Reading Society of Corfu**, a traditional building with a very lovely internal staircase. Here one also finds the church of the **Virgin Mary Antivounitssa** which houses the Byzantine Museum (see chapter museums).

The **church of the Panagia Antivouniotissa**, one of the oldest and most important post-Byzantine churches in Corfu town, was built in the 15th century in the style of the Septinsular basilicas. The church ceiling is divided into sections, magnificently decorated with woodcarvings and gilded elements. Natural light flows into the church through the large semicircular windows on its long sides.

The icon screen of the Panagia Antivouniotissa.

The walls are covered by impressive illustrated tapestries and the church's stone icon screen dates to the 17th century. In the outer narthex tombstones can be found with the coats-of-arms of the nobles buried here as well as traces of wall paintings. The name Antivouniotissa comes from the hill of Antivouni or Oreovouni (today's Kabielo), upon which the church stands.

The imposing building located just before the street turns is the **old Prefecture**. A plaque informs you that John Kapodistrias (1776 -1831) the first

Mouragia with the old Prefecture building at the edge.

The square with the church
of Panagia Spiliotissa.

Governor of Greece was born there. The Prefecture building, which houses a part of the University of the Ionian, is an exceptional example of the ruling architectural movement of the 19th century. It was built in 1840 on the plans of the local architect Chronis. Below the road is the **Gate of St. Nicolas**, an impressive remnant of the old fortifications. Continuing along the waterfront street you will pass the **Metropolitan Mansion**. Here you are literally walking on the fortifications facing the sea. Soon you will see to your right the **old harbor**.

The **Cathedral, Panayia Spiliotissa** (Our Lady of the Cave), lies to the southwest above the Old Harbor. Μερικά σκαλοπάτια οδηγούν στην είσοδο της εκκλησίας, που κοιτάει προς το λιμάνι. The church is dedicated to three saints: to Panagia Spiliotissa, as after the destruction of the church of that name the Panagia's icon was brought here; to Saint Vlassios, whose church had earlier stood on this site; and to Saint Theodora, whose relic has been housed within the church ever since it arrived on Corfu from Constantinople along with the relic of Saint Spyridon (see page 42, Saints of Corfu). The church is dated to 1577 and has interesting icons of the Ionian School and some older Byzantine icons, such as the 15th-century icon of Panagia Demosiana, which is said to have been made in Ioannina and is painted on both sides. There are also other works by Damaskinos, Tzannes and Paramythiotis. The metropolitan church is in the style of the three-aisled Septinsular churches whilst its impressive facade stands out for its renaissance features.

The Cathedral (Panayia Spiliotissa)

The gate of Ayios Georgios.

The old Town of Corfu and the Old Fortress. Aerial photograph. Also visible are the church of Agios Georgios at Spianada, the area between the town and the fortress.

The New Fortress

info

A permanent exhibition of Ceramic Art is housed in the Fortress barracks (see Museums). In the summer musical, theatrical and folklore events are sometimes held in the precinct of the building.

This lion is located on the south bastion of Skarponas and is characterised by its very short muzzle. The inscription commemorates the completion of the wall on the order of the governor and captain of Corfu Benedictus Erizzo, who was responsible for the building works in 1583.

The elevation above the Old Harbor is the best place to get a view of the New Fortress (Fortezza Nuova) which is open to visitors and which plays host to the Greek Navy, among other things. The New Fortress was built between 1570 and 1580 during the general refortification of Corfu. The main architect was Francisco Vitelli who demolished approximately 2,000 houses and churches as well as one the most beautiful gates in the town, Porta Reale, to get the building material he required. By the end of the 17th century the defense of the New Fortress was supplemented by the garrisons of Avrami and Sorroko. However, a large part of the New Fortress was destroyed after the demands of the Great Powers before the union of the Ionian islands with Greece but also by the heavy bombing raids during World War II.

Today you can still admire its beautiful entrance. Observe its marvellous entrance with the Lion of St. Mark on the upper part. The Gate of Spilia can be found in the area behind the port. This is one of the two gates of the old town walls that have survived and which ensured communication between the town and the new port. The gate was built in the 16th century and was the main entrance to the sea.

Panoramic view of the New Fortress.

The churches of Corfu town

Agios Ioannis Prodromos
(St John the Baptist)

This church is located on N. Theotokis Street and was built in the 15th century (1480). Its characteristic features are the belfry with the perforated walls, the peaked rook, the ceiling painted by S. Sperantzas in 1773 and the pulpit. The marble icon screen is adorned with famous works by Georgios Chrysolaras, Tzenos and Emmanuel Tzannes. The church also holds a reliquary with the relics of Saints John Chrysostom and John Damascene. The church celebrates the feast day of St John the Baptist on 29 August.

Agios Antonios and Agios Andreas
(St Anthony and St Andrew)

This church is located at the corner of N. Theotokis Street and Palaiologou Street and was built on the site of an older church in 1753. The church is in the Septinsular ecclesiastical type of a single-aisled basilica, and its characteristic feature is the groin vault roof. There is a fine marble icon screen that was made by the architect Alexandros Trivolis-Pierris approximately twenty years after the construction of the church.

Church of the Pantokrator

This church was built in either the middle or the end of the 16th century and it is located in Taxiarchon Square in the district of Kabielo. It belongs to the Septinsular ecclesiastical type of a single-aisled basilica with a wood and tile roof and has an exonarthex only in its north section. A characteristic feature is the sculpted angel, by the 18th-century sculptor Toretti, at the peak of the roof. Only certain sections remain today of the perforated belfry. The marble icon screen inside the church, with works by the icon painter Chrysolaras, is particularly fine.

Panagia Tenedou Monastery (Blessed Virgin of the Carmelites)

This monastery is located outside of the New Fortress and is essentially a Catholic church construction of which began in 1678. Its baroque architectural style is particularly emphasised, particularly on the dome and in the sculpted Venetian lion over the central entrance. The church played host to the first printing press in Greek lands in 1798 and, in 1800, to the island's first public library. Moreover, the first Greek public school was opened in the church in 1805, its director being Ioannis Kapodistrias. The church celebrates its feast day on 16 July.

Monastery of San Francesco

This Catholic monastery was built in the early 13th century, with the oldest section and the chapel of San Angelo dating to this century, although they have been significantly altered. The central *katholikon* church of the Monastery survives today, with repairs from the 17th-18th century and a monastic courtyard and portico. A few interesting decorative features still survive on the side of the cloister.

Agioi Pateres and Agios Arsenios
(Holy Fathers and Saint Arsenios)

This 15th-century church is located on the corner of Agion Pateron and Agias Varvaras Streets. Its facade, with the Tuscan Doric pillars, is reminiscent of late baroque Venetian monuments. Its interior decoration features mascarons (sculpted stone heads). There are plans for this church to be converted into the Ecclesiastical Museum of Corfu.

Anountsiata

This monument is of Europe-wide significance, as it was here that the Latin nobles who fell at the Battle of Lepanto in 1571 are buried. This naval battle - the greatest that humankind had known up till then - marked the end to the Ottoman threat and was the first time that the Christian powers had emerged victorious after eight great battles at sea in which they had been defeated. After the church was destroyed by German bombardments on 14 September 1943, the bones were transferred to the Catholic cemetery of Corfu in the district of Kapoukinoi. Today only the belfry and a part of the sanctuary survive.

The square
(*plakada* of the saint) and church of Agios Spyridon

Leaving Spianada by **Nikiforou Theotoki street**, which begins just behind the Liston, somewhere near the middle where the buildings are separated, you will observe the characteristic vaulted streets. These vaults, the so-called "voltas" contain more building space while at the same time protecting pedestrians from the sun and the rain.

In some of the narrower streets the top floors of the houses on each side of the street nearly touch each other but down on the street there is still plenty of room for one to walk about.

A beautiful and lively square can be found along Nikiphorou Theotoki Street, the square of the church of Agios Spyridon. The locals call this square 'plakada t'Agiou', as the church of Agios Spyridon acts as a kind of informal town cathedral. In the summer the square is filled with painters and artists. In the centre of the square is the statue of Georgios Theotokis (1844-1916), a Corfiot politician who served as prime minister of Greece four times in the late 19th to early 20th centuries.

Agios Spyridon Square (Iroon Kypriakou Agona Square) with the statue of Nikiphoros Theotokis and the church of the Panagia Faneromeni ton Xenon

Around the square, which was once known as Sternon Square or Del Banco, are two other important Orthodox churches: **Panagia Xenon (Kyra Faneromeni)** and **Agios Ioannis Prodromos**. The church of the Hyperagia Theotokou Faneromeni, or Panagia Xenon, was built by Ieronymous Nikodemos and has three aisles. Its characteristic features include the ceiling, painted by N. Koutouzis (18th century) and the icon screen, one of the most impressive decorated church icon screens in Corfu. Scholars are unanimous that the doors of the icon screen as being of unique artistic value. The icon of the Tree of Jesse is particularly splendid, with small images of the prophets and their sayings relating to the coming of the Messiah.

Agios Spyridon Lane is one of the main commercial routes and one of the oldest streets in Corfu town. This historic street has acted as the commercial backbone of the town from early on.

The historic building of the Ionian Bank and Banknote Museum.

The Square is also the location of the fine **Ionian Bank** building containing the **Banknote Museum** (see Museums), designed by the leading Corfiot architect Ioannis Chronis. It was one of the first bank buildings in Greece and its construction began in 1844. The historic building of the Ionian Bank is a monumental structure with hewn masonry on the ground floor and elaborate pedimental decoration on the roof and storeys. It is styled as an Ionian temple with arched windows.

On Michali Theotoki Street we encounter the paved **Vrachlotis Square** with the Vrachlotis Cistern, a copy of a Venetian original. It is in this Square that the mastello custom, with a barrel or cylindrical trough for washing clothes, is held at Easter.

The Square, or *plakada*, of Agios Spyridon can be found a little further up on the right, on Nikiphorou Theotoki Street, with the **church of Agios Spyridon** at the far end.

The original church of St. Spyridonas was in the Sarokkos area but it was necessary to demolish it for the building of the walls. The present church was erected in 1590. The church itself is a typical religious edifice found throughout the Ionian islands. The roof of Saint Spyridonas is divided into 17 sections, trimmed in gold - which are the original ones - and the icons deal with events in the saint's life, the Four Evangelists and similar motifs and the iconostasis is of marble. The holy relic of the saint is kept in a silver sarcophagus from the 19th century, on the right side of the church.

As for the paintings within the church, it must be noted that the icon painters from the Ionian Island School were not only familiar with the Renaissance but influenced by it. The ceiling of Saint Spyridonas was originally made by Panayiotis Doxaras (1662-1729) who had served his apprenticeship in Rome and Venice and was a great admirer of Tintoretto, Titian and Veronese. He was also the founder the Ionian School which one finds throughout the Ionian islands.

The original icons and other religious paintings by Doxaras were destroyed by damp and were replaced in the middle of there 19th century by copies made by N. Aspiotis. In the rest of Greece the Byzantine models have always been strictly adhered to, even today, but on the Ionian islands there has been a strong and lasting influence of the Italian art of the 17th century, and the churches tend to be long and low with very impressive bell-towers. The belfry of Saint Spyridonas is very reminiscent of the Greek Church of Ayios Georgios in Venice which was built during approximately the same period.

The reliquary and holy relic of Saint Spyridon
The reliquary in which the holy relic of Saint Spyridon is kept was made in Vienna in 1867, a silver reliquary with emerald decoration. The Saint's holy relic remained in Cyprus for around 300 years after his death, until it was transferred to Constantinople in the late 7th century AD to protect it from the Arab raids against the island. In 1456, three years after the fall of Constantinople to the Ottomans, the priest Grigorios Polyeuktos took the holy relic of the saint, along with the relics of Saint Theodora the Augusta, to Epirus and from there to Corfu, where he bequeathed the holy relics to the priest Georgios Kalochairetis.

Ayios Spyridonas (St. Spyridonas)

St. Spyridonas was the Bishop of Cyprus and took part in the First Ecumenical Synod of Nicea in 325 where he condemned heresy. After his death, his relics were kept at Constantinople and when the capital of Byzantium fell to the Turks, a number of refugees took his remains with them. The relics reached Corfu in 1489. We have no precise idea of how he became so closely identified with the fate of the island until he was known as Ayios Spyridonas, patron saint of Corfu but the tradition that states he saved the island from plague dates from 1553. It is also believed that he saved Corfu from pestilence in 1630 and 1673 and from the Turks in 1716. Tradition relates that he appeared dressed as a monk holding a torch and spread panic among the Turkish forces. The saint's feast day (December 12) is celebrated with particular pomp on Corfu. Many boys have been given his name and the expression "In the name of St. Spyridon" with the characteristic lilting local accent, is heard constantly.

Four times a year (on August 11, the first Sunday in November, Palm Sunday and Holy Saturday) services are held and the holy relics are carried in procession about the town in commemoration of the saint's miracle working feats. These services are accompanied by bands from the entire island which are all noteworthy which one comes to expect from an island with such a long and esteemed musical tradition.

The icon screen and belfry of Agios Spyridon.

Kabielo

This is the oldest quarter in the Old Town and is located to the north of Saint Spyridonas. If you follow Philarmonikis St. and go up the stairs you will find yourself in Kabielo which has many narrow lanes and alleyways, high traditional Corfiot buildings and small rather quaint squares. This old quarter of the town is a rather miraculous place where one can easily lose himself in large part because the street lay-out is rather labyrinthian.

Characteristic lane of Kabielo with, on the right, Kremasti Square and its Venetian fountain.

Agia Eleni Square with its beautiful palm tree.

Small squares, churches tucked away in corners, with washing hanging over lines attached to houses facing each other across the streets has a flavor all its own, unique in Greece. **Kremasti Square** is one of the most beautiful in Kabielo, with the lovely fountain at its centre. The elegant mouth of the fountain, with its relief decoration, was donated to the Community by Antonios Kokkinis in 1669. The **church of Panagia Kremasti** is also to be found in this Square, built in Septinsular style. Its interior is particularly grand, with a marble screen the doors of which are decorated in a vine leaf motif, stone pews and huge, impressive icons by Sperantzas (18th century).

Another old and historic square, the largest in Kabielo, is that with the **church of the Taxiarchon Michail and Gavril** (Archangels Michael and Gabriel), with its impressive marble entranceway. This square is located at the heart of Kabielo. From Taxiarchon Square, charming Dousman Street leads us to the **church of San Nicolo dei Vecchi**. This was one of the richest churches of Kabielo and its impressive chancel screen one of the oldest preserved in a Corfu church. Lastly, we come to **Agia Eleni or Kyropoulas Square**, which takes us into the lanes of Kabielo and Dousman Street and with a palm tree at its centre, more reminiscent of a charming inner courtyard than a public square.

Townhall Square

The Catholic church of SS Iakovos and Christophoros (Duomo)

If you follow Michael Theotoki St. in a while you will reach Evgeniou Voulgareos St. which begins on the southern end of the Liston. On the left-hand corner as you enter Voulgareos, is the Town Hall. Originally, the Town Hall was the stoa of the Corfiot nobles, the "loggia nobili" and is the only building in town that has carved stone masonry. Its construction began in 1663 and lasted for thirty years. It was built from hewn Sinion rock in a Renaissance style with subjects from the life and mythology of the island and is the only building in Corfu town with carved masonry. Its two central sides are decorated with stone masks and various historical inscriptions and symbols. The bust that ornaments the southern is that of the Venetian Fleet Commander Franceso Morosini (1619 -1694). In 1721 the stoa became a theater and later operas were also performed there. The transformation of the building into the Town Hall of Corfu was done at the beginning of the 20th century when a separate building was constructed for the opera which was levelled by the bombing raids of World War II. During that period another floor was added but without harming in any way the harmonious proportions of the edifice.

The open area in front of the Town Hall is framed by two other important Venetian buildings: one of them is the Roman Catholic **Cathedral of St. Iako-**

Views of the interior and exterior of the church of SS Iakovos and Christophoros.

vos (1665) which has been renovated. The central altar is dedicated to the Crucified Christ whilst the three chapels of Saint Spyridon and Saint Arsenios, the Immaculate Conception of the Virgin and the Mystery of the Holy Eucharist are on the right. To the right of these are the chapels of Christ the King of the Universe, Our Lady of Health and Saint Therese of Lisieux. The Catholic Cathedral contains a number of splendid works of art, including the wall painting of Saint Chrysolaras from 1756.

The **residence of the Roman Catholic archbishop** (17th century) which later became the courthouse and today is one of the branches of the Bank of Greece. This building was one of the most important public works encircling Dimarchiou Square, which was the town's social and cultural centre during the Venetian period. The elegant building has a simple facade with its central axis emphasised by the ornate entrance stairway, and a central balcony with the characteristic balustrade of the elaborate marble railings. During the time of Venetian rule this area must have been the center of social life on Corfu. The statue of Iakovos Polylalas still stands in Dimarchiou Square. Polylalas was a distinguished student and publisher of Dionysios Solomos and an author and translator most famous for his art criticism.

The Ionian Parliament was built by Ioannis Chronis in 1855 and is located in Dimarchiou Square. The building is in a neoclassical style with Doric columns at the entrance and inscriptions in Greek and English on both sides. After the union of the Ionian Islands with Greece the building was appropriated by the Greek state and made into a church, whilst in 1978 it was renovated and converted into a museum dedicated to the struggles for freedom of the Ionian Islands.

In Theatre Square (Townhall square) the present day Town Hall which house the Loggia and later the town's theater. Right: The Catholic church of St. Iakovos can be see, a typical example from the Venetian occupation.

THE NEW TOWN

Sarokko Square

The new town is comprised of the neighbourhoods of San Rocco (Sarocco), Garitsa, Mandoukio, Kefalomandouko and Anemomyli. It also includes the districts of Kanoni, Analipseos, Palioupoli, Neratzicha, the airport, Sotiros hill, Kotsela, the former Community of Evropouloi, Potamos, and the Potamos salt marshes, which will be described below.

After the Town Hall you continue along Voulgareos St. You reach a small square where Theotoki St. begins, the main commercial street in the town which ends at **Sarokko Square**. At approximately the midway point of this street, to your left, is the new **Municipal Theater** and behind it, the Prefecture building and the offices of OTE (Phone Company). The new town, outside the walls has always had as its center Sarokko Square (Y. Theotoki). This is also where the buses leave for the nearby villages.

From Sarokko Square one can also take a very pleasant stroll, turning left at Alexandras Avenue (where the Post Office is also located), a tree-lined street with wealthy homes which ends at the avenue along the waterfront, **Garitsas**. From there you can go to the Archaeological Museum (see chapter museums) to get an idea of the artistic treasures of ancient Corfu. Just a little further down you will encounter the **Obelisk** (1841) built in honor of Sir Howard Douglas (1776 -1861), a distinguished theoretician on military science who was the High Commissioner of the Ionian islands from 1835-1840. Douglas wrote the first technical manual on the uses of naval bombardment.

Platyteras Monastery

The Monastery is located a short distance from the new port near Sarocco Square. It was founded in 1743 by the Lefkadiot monk Chrysanthos Syropoulos. The Kapodistrias family, especially Ioannis, Greece's first Governor, had close relations with the Monastery and acted as its benefactor in various ways. Ioannis Kapodistrias' grave as well as that of Tzavelas, a hero of the Greek War of Independence, is to be found within the Monastery. The interior of the church is rich, with fine icons by splendid artists (Kantounis, Koutouzis), a gold-inlaid wood-carved icon screen, a variety of important 17th-century icons by Tzannes, Poulakis and Klontzas and valuable holy relics. The pyramidical domed belfry from 1864 rises above the central entrance. The Monastery celebrates its feast day on 15 August, the feast of Dormition of the Virgin.

The monument of Menekrates dates to around 600 BC. It bears an archaic inscription of ten lines, one of the oldest extant ancient Greek inscriptions.

Menecrates monument

Behind the Obelisk, in the courtyard of the Police Station, is the Monument to Menecrates. The surrounding area was once the ancient cemetery and this monument is in honor of a man who was not buried here but perished at sea. The inscription, on the upper part of the circular monument, which dates it to around 600 B.C., is in Archaic writing and is read from right to left. It tells us that Menecrates was the consul from Corfu to his birthplace, in Oianthia, near Galaxidi. The monument was found in 1843 and there are some who maintain that it was crowned by the lion which is on display in the museum.

The road continues on along the sea, a very pleasant promenade with a lovely view of the Fortress. The south end of this bay is called Anemomylos and after that begins the Kanoni headland.

Panoramic view of the new town from Garitsa bay and the port.

Get to know the island

The island of Corfu lies in the Ionian Sea between Greece and Italy. The brilliance of the former and the beauty of the latter are clearly recorded in this place, small though it may be. There are villages which climb to the slopes of Mt Pantokrator, and others under the olive and cypress trees through which one can walk down to pretty coves or sndy beaches. The task of describing the beauty and history of Corfu is a difficult one. It becomes still harder when the description has to be crammed into the limited pages of a guide-book. In our effort to convey as effectively as possible the history, natural beauty, culture and life-style of this island and its inhabitants. we have divided our tour of it into five routes.

THE TEN MOST BEAUTIFUL PARTS OF THE ISLAND THAT YOU MUST DEFINITELY VISIT

1. Old town
2. Palaiokastritsa
3. Peroulades
4. Pelekas (Throne of the Kaiser)
5. Sidari - Canal d'Amour
6. Myrtiotissa Monastery
7. Kerasia Beach
8. Vlacherna - Pontikonisi
9. Mount Pantokrator
10. Diapontia Islands

Route One
Pages 94-103

KANONI PENINSULA
Ancient Corfu, Temple of Artemis, Kanoni, Panagia Vlacherna, Pontikonisi, Mon Repos, Palaiopoli

Route Two
Pages 104-117

NORTHWEST OF THE TOWN
Palaiokastritsa, Palaiokastritsa Monastery, Lakones, Angelokastro
SOUTHWEST OF THE TOWN
Agioi Deka, Ai Gordis, Kynopiastes, Sinarades, Pelekas, Glyfada, Kontogialos, Ermones, Myrtidiotissa Monastery, Ropas Valley

Route Three
Pages 118-133

Potamos Salt Marshes, Kontokali, Gouvia, Dasia, Kato and Ano Korakiana, Ypsos, Pantokrator Mountain and Monastery, Agios Markos, Spartylas, Strinillas, Petaleia, Barbati, Nisaki, Kalami, Kouloura, Agios Stephanos Sinion, Kassiopi, Peritheia, Antinioti Lagoon, Acharavi

Route Four
Pages 134-141

Roda, Agios Georgios Pagon, Arillas, Sidari, Peroulades, Agios Stephanos Avlioton

Route Five
Pages 142-151

Perama, Gastouri, Benitses, Moraitika, Mesongi, Chlomos, Agios Georgios Argyradon, Korission Lagoon, Argyrades, Marathias, Perivoli, Kavos, Arkoudilas, Spartera, Gardiki, Agios Matthaios

Route One

KANONI PENINSULA
Ancient Corfu, Temple of Artemis,
Kanoni, Panagia Vlacherna, Pontikonisi,
Mon Repos, Palaiopoli

Introduction On Route One you will be able to experience the unique beauty of Kanoni, famous for its view, the islet with Vlacherna Monastery, the celebrated Pontikonisi with Pantokrator Monastery, the ancient town of Corfu and the temple of Artemis. During this short tour the visitor has the chance to not only enjoy the site where the most important events in the island's ancient history have taken place but to truly get to know and be enchanted by a landscape that has always inspired local and foreign artists, to become better acquainted with the ecclesiastical art of Corfu as this has achieved its definitive form in the churches and monasteries and to be deeply moved by an area where the the Great Powers clashed but where the victor was once again the people of Corfu.

KANONI PENINSULA

Ancient Corfu

Temple of Artemis

Heading south from the town and passing the installations of the Naval Society on your left you will go downhill and take the coast road along the **bay of Garitsa**. Near the end of this bay you pass the road to the airport (3 km.) on the right and the road to the left that you will come back on and continue on, going uphill.

Now you are in the area of **ancient Corfu**. The landscape has radically changed since antiquity. Then the bay of Garitsa extended much further to the west and ended at a harbor, called Alkinoos, one of the two the town possessed. Thus the ancient town which was founded in the 8th century B.C. was located on a headland between two harbors: the harbor of Alkinoos and Yllaikos harbor which was located on the Chaikoipoulos salt lake, an area that has since been filled in and is where the airport is found. The harbor of Alkinoos had a narrow entrance with two towers guarding it. Remnants of the eastern tower have been found.

You will continue to ascend the hill. The north side of the cape was protected by walls which began at the end of the harbor of Alkinoos and a section of them have survived near the present-day cemetery and at the **monastery of Ayioi Theodori**

Opposite page: Magical Pontikonisi and Panagia Vlacherna Monastery.

Halkiopoulos Lagoon

This lagoon continues to function as an important wetland, hosting rare species of migrating birds despite the tourism development in the area and the expansion of the airport. A significant number of rare birds can be observed during the migration period, such as the great egret, a species that is threatened with extinction. There is commercial fishing over the 200 hectares of the lagoon, which covers the island's large demand for fish.

(Sts. Theodore). The only reason that this section of the wall survived was that a Byzantine chapel was there. It consists of a tower six meters high and the locals have called the it **Tower of Nereantzichas**.

Near this region you can see the few traces of the **temple of Artemis Gorgous**, one of the earliest Doric stone temples. This archaic limestone temple was built in circa 590 BC, with seventeen columns along each of its long sides and eight along its short sides. The west pediment (now in the Archaeological Museum) was found in the archaeological site along with a giant altar, which gives us an idea of the size of the original building. The relief pediment is one of the few surviving works of the late archaic period. The temple was discovered during fortress works by the French in 1812, when a section of the ancient aqueduct was also revealed.

After passing the houses that dot the slopes of Analipsi hill the road continues on until it reaches a square which has a splendid view. A view which is, to a degree, the "trademark" of Corfu. Kanoni lies above a small square, next to a tourist pavilion. The French Republicans set up a military battery there in 1798. It is one of the most beautiful landscapes on the islands and thrills all visitors. No traveller should miss the experience of enjoying this enchanting and totally unique site no matter the time of day.

During the day there are its reflections of light and early evening with the unique sunset the site offers and of course its magic in moonlight. In front of you and a little to the right is the entrance to Yllaikos harbor which during antiquity was protected by this and a fence. Now there is a narrow bridge there which ends at Perama.

The airport and Halkiopoulos lagoon at Kanoni.

Panayia Vlacheron Pontikonisi

info

Pontikonisi lies 800 metres from the coast. You can reach Vlacherna Monastery on foot from the Kanoni rise, where there are small boats that sail to Pontikonisi. The boat will take you there for a fee of €2 per person, and the bus as far as Kanoni costs €1 per person.

Left: Interior view of Panagia Vlacherna.
Right: The church of the Metamorphosis of the Soter at Pontikonisi.

The landscape is complemented by two islets on the left, each with its own monastery. The monastery on the nearest island which one can reach along an elevated path is dedicated to the Panayia ton Vlacheron and the one on Pontikonisi is dedicated to the Pantokrator.

The bright-white **Monastery of Panagia Vlacherna** dates to the 17th century. To enter, you must pass through an arch underneath the belfry which leads to a small courtyard from which you can enter the church. The church is dedicated to the Metamorphosis of the Soter and celebrates its feast day on the day of the Metamorphosis, 6 August. Only on this day is it permitted to visit the island in pilgrimage: on other days you can only visit momentarily and must immediately leave the rock.

Pontikonisi according to the interpretation found in Homer's *Odyssey* is the ship of Odysseus that Poseidon turned to a stone. The Byzantine chapel dating to the 11th or 12th century at the peak of the island contains memorial plaques commemorating the visit of Empress Elisabeth of the Austria and Archduke Rudolph in 1800.

Mon Repos
Palaiopoli

Leaving Kanoni and returning to Corfu you pass through an area full of tourist establishments, one of the most heavily visited parts of the island during the summer which lies right outside the airport. You take a turn-off to the right which leads to the top of Analypsi hill. The largest part of the top of the hill, where the acropolis of ancient Corfu was located, is occupied by th istallations of **Mon Repos** (see page 66, museums). In the center of this estate lies the mansion that was built in 1824 for High Commissioner Sir Frederic Adam and then became part of the holdings of th Greek royal family. The Duke of Edinburgh was born there in 1921. Opposite the entrance to Mon Repos are found the ruins of the Early Christain **church of Ayia Kerkyra** (St. Corfu) the **basilica of Palaiopolis** which was certainly built before 450 A.D. using matrial taken from ancient structures and has been rebuilt many times since then after being destroyed by invaders. It was most recently destroyed during the bombardment in 1940. The Inscription over the west entrance refers to the founding of the church by Bishop Hovian of Corfu after he had destroyed the pagan altars on the island. It is a five-aisled basilica with a transept, a semi-circular apse to the east and two narthexes in the west. Mosaics dating to the 5th and 6th centuries AD were found in the south aisle, the narthex and the northwest annex. Birds, fish and fruits are the dominant decorative motifs. Sections from the mosaic floor and several other finds from the church can be seen on display in the Byzantine Museum.

Mon Repos is a typical English villa, a work of the British architect Whitmore. It is a single building with a simple design, large doors and windows and a typical application of the English 'classical' tradition with the addition of some Greek elements and palladiums. The School of Fine Arts was installed here in 1833, with Pavlos Prosalentis as its director. In 1864 the building and gardens were granted to then King George I for his own use, and he renamed in Mon Repos. Since then until 1967 it was used by the former Greek royal family as their summer residence, and was the birthplace of Prince Philip, husband of Queen Elizabeth II. Today it can be visited by the public and was recently converted into a museum.

The five-aisled basilica of Palaiopoli was built in the 5th century AD by Bishop Iovanos over the ruins of a Roman Odeon. Two fluted Corinthian columns survive at its entrance. Along this road, which ended at one of the gates of the ancient city, there is a number of grave monuments from the ancient cemetery.

Most of the remnants of ancient Corfu are to be found amid the lush vegetation of Mon Repos. Among these ruins is the town's largest temple, a structure that was rebuilt in the 4th century B.C. and was perhaps dedicated to Hera. This temple is mentioned by Thuycidides.

If you continue on up to the top of the hill you will be able to visit the **Temple of Kardakios** another Doric structure very little of which has survived. The temple was perhaps dedicated to Apollo and was discovered by chance in 1822 by British soldiers who were digging in search of water because the Kardakios spring which supplied most of the passing ships, had suddenly gone dry. The eastern side of the temple has fallen into the sea.

The view from the top of the hill is magnificent and one can see a large part of the Mon Repos estate as well as its harbor.

Ruins of the temple of Hera.

Returing, you go downhill and arrive at the sourthermost point of Garitsa bay. This is where the **church of the Saints Jason and Sosipatros** is located, one of the most beautiful Byzantine monuments on Corfu and indeed one of the few structures from the period that have survived. The saints to whom the church is dedicated are considered to be the ones who brought Christianity to the island and according to tradition Sosipatros was martyred here during the time of Caligula. Both of them were disciples of St. Paul.

Their church is dated to the 11th century if one can judge from the wall painting of St. Artemis on the eastern wall of the narthex. This same building has three ancient columns each one carved from a single piece of rock. The icons of the two saints are the work of the hagiographer Emmanuel Tzane from the end of the 16th century, one of the leading representatives of the Cretan School.

The temple of SS Iasonas and Sosipatros, one of the most beautiful Byzantine monuments of Corfu.

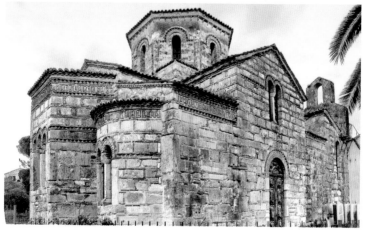

Panagia Vlacherna and Pontikonisi.

Route Two

NORTHWEST OF THE TOWN
Palaiokastritsa, Palaiokastritsa Monastery,
Lakones, Angelokastro
SOUTHWEST OF THE TOWN
Agioi Deka, Ai Gordis, Kynopiastes, Sinarades,
Pelekas, Glyfada, Kontogialos, Ermones,
Myrtidiotissa Monastery, Ropas Valley

Introduction The western coastline of central Corfu is an area so rich in images and history that every landscape is a living example of the coexistence of nature and ancient and modern monuments in complete harmony, tourism with peaceful farming villages, the beautiful open sea with the lacy coastline and the superb beaches which are bursting with life each summer. Nature has ornamented these coastlines with truly unique gems, the best being perhaps the triple bay of Palaiokastritsa which according to myth was where the town of the Phaecaenas was where Odysseus made his last stop before his return to Ithaca. But history has also added this own special brushstroke, the imposing Angelokastro, the nearly impregnable castle the ruins of which still cling to the enormous rock in seeming readiness to resist any invaders through the resistance of time. Further to the south, the picturesqueness and the delightful colors of Palakas, the beauty of the beaches at Ermones at yet another touch to the landscape and a certain sense of equilibrium.

Palaiokastritsa combines beautiful beaches with lots of greenery.
Opposite page: panoramic view of Palaiokastritsa beach.

NORTHWEST OF THE TOWN

Palaiokastritsa

The area of Palaiokastritsa, which lies 25. km. from the town consists of two headlands and five small coves. The landscape is so beautiful that Palaiokastritsa was one of the first places on the island to be touristically developed. Despite all the hotels and the holiday residences that have sprung up the landscape above the coves which are divided from each other by steep cliffs, continues to be completely enchanting. The road winds its way down toward the large beach. To its left, paths head off to even smaller beaches where one can have a swim. There is also a tiny harbor here, in the bay of Antypas, where fishing boats anchor and yachts pass by. The underwater world is hugely attractive to spear fisherman and divers.

info

Location: Palaiokastritsa is twenty minutes by car from Corfu town.
Type: Beach with sand and pebbles.
Services: Many accommodation options, such as hotels and rented rooms and apartments. Some shops along the length of the road, such as a small supermarket, bakery, bars, travel agencies and souvenir shops. Sun umbrellas and recliners for hire along most of the beaches and the main beaches have showers.
Activities: Rent a boat and see the caves along the coast from up close and travel to the other beaches that are accessible only by sea. Perfect for snorkelling enthusiasts.
Features: The water in this region is cold as it gushes down quicker and there are cold streams.

Liapades beach.

Liapades and Doukades

Liapades is one of Corfu's traditional villages, located close to Palaiokastritsa and famed for the wine produced by the kakotrygis grape variety. You can have a wonderful swim at Liapades beach, which is sandy with a few pebbles and surrounded by much greenery and refreshing waters. Alternatively, hire a boat and visit the neighbouring beaches and a small cave on the left edge of the beach. A panoramic road that traverses the village of Lakones allows you to admire all of Palaiokastritsa from up high and have an overview of all the beaches, steep cliffs and the two islets with Mediterranean vegetation, olive trees, cypresses and lemon trees that scramble down to the beach.

Doukades is close by, and of interest here are the renovated stone mansion of the Theotokis family, the Venetian-style building of Kouartanos, the Korangos estate and the Elementary School at the entrance to the village. Both villages have been declared traditional settlements.

Picturesque corners in Doukades.

Palaiokastritsa Monastery

Located on the north headland of the area on top of a cliff is the Palaiokastritsa Monastery, founded in 1225. The Monastery was built on this site after the icon of the Hyperagia Virgin was found here. Its name of Palaiokastritsa comes from a natural castle (*kastro*) that functioned as the bastion of this then inhabited region. The central building of the church is located in the middle of the complex, which is comprised of courtyards, cells, porticos, facilities for the monks, olive oil presses and storage areas. The present building is from the 18th-19th century. But internally the modern edifice is a superb example of Greek monastic architecture. The *katholikon* church of the Monastery is single-aisled and contains a number of fine icons, primarily in the Cretan style. The belfry is attached to its northeast corner. The church ceiling is the result of a unique architectural design. A central point is the presence of the wood-carved Tree of Life. Within the Monastery there are some fine icons, primarily in the Cretan style and dating from the 15th to the 18th centuries. The Monastery has a small Museum with Byzantine and post-Byzantine icons, holy books, vessels and ritual vestments, as well as the skeleton of a prehistoric mammoth in the central Room. The main exhibits are the icon of the Dormition of the Virgin, covered with silver inlay and the silver-bound Bible decorated with precious stones. The Greek Orthodox ritual and the legendary sea monster are two representations which are also well worth seeing. Outside the Monastery there is an old canon from the artillery kept here by the French garrison (from 1797-1799 and 1807-1814). The view from the Monastery is wonderful and in the forefront we can see the little islet of Kolovri, which well deserves the title of Odysseus' petrified ship.

Lakones

Picturesque lane at Lakones.

You go back to the turn-off to Lakones.You leave the main road and go right uphill amid olive groves. The olives trees of Corfu have a size that is seldom found in the rest of Greece and that is why travelling through Corfu you have the impression your are moving through an endless forest. Here is also another place to admire the terraces that have been built on the slopes so the hills could be cultivated. The tillers of the soil removed the small stones from the ground and in that way created a rather flat space where the olive trees could be planted and other crops grown around them. At the same time, with the stones that were taken away walls were built to keep the soil from being washed away by the winter rains. As you continue to ascend a marvellous landscape opens before you revealing Palaiokastritsa with its coves.

Lakones (25 km.) is a picturesque village on the slopes of a mountain with a marvellous view to the south. One of the sites that lies outside the village is called Bella Vista. There are very pleasant cafes there where one can sit and enjoy the view. For the more venturesome, there is a steep path that leads down to Palaiokastritsa.

Angelokastro

After Lakones, with the cliff always on your left you will see Angelokastro for the first time a Byzantine fortress situated on what appears to be an inaccessible hilltop.I n order to reach the castle you follow the road as far as the village of **Krini**. Stop here to drink some water from the cold spring that gushes out in the small village square or to order a coffee from the neighbouring cafe, until the sun goes down a little so that the route up to Angelokastro will be more relaxing.

At the turn-off to the village you continue on left until you reach the base of the hill and then begin to climb the steep and narrow path. There is a panoramic view from the peak on which the castle sits that even includes the town of Corfu.

Angelokastro was the westernmost outpost of the Despotate of Epirus, one of the Greek Orthodox hegemonies which had come to prevail in the western Balkans and the dominance of Byzantium began to want during the Middle Ages (13th century). The castle was also known as Castle Michel Angelo thus retaining the name of its creator Michael II the Despot of Epirus. The castle sits on a rock 609 m. high which is surrounded by the sea with only a narrow channel connecting it to the mainland. At the top is a small chapel to the Archangels and on its northwestern wall is a shrine to Ayia Kyriaki set in a cave. The position of the castle was very important during the early years of the Venetian occupation until the end of the 16th cen-

info

Until it was abandoned during the Venetian period, the fortress of Angelokastro had been unassailable. At its peak is the little church of the Archangels Michael and Gabriel and an hermitage, whilst near the northwest wall is a cave with the holy altar of Saint Kyriaki. It is open daily from 8:30 to 15:00.

tury. The Governor, who was elected by the Corfiot Senate had his seat there which only further proves how powerful a position it held.

One of the most dramatic incidents in the history of the castle was played out during the Turkish invasion of 1571. The villagers from the surrounding areas had taken refuge in the castle and thus were in a position to turn back the invaders from the beginning. Before leaving the castle if you descend a few steps in the left hand corner you will find the cell of a hermit and a pilgrimage site.

The village of **Makrades**, famed for its traditional shops with produce such as honey and oregano, lies close to Angelokastro.

In the past Angelokastro had been selected as a lookout point for pirates and an exceptional point from which to ward off enemy attacks, such as that by the Turks in 1571, who tried in vain to lay siege. Given its height and location, there is a wonderful panoramic view from the castle and, when the sky is clear, you can see as far as Corfu town.

SOUTHWEST OF THE TOWN

Leaving the town you go past the airport. This circular tour, approximately 32 kilometers long takes you to the south and west of Corfu and combines beaches with places that have a panoramic view. This area, a part of the "Middle" of the island can also be reached from Palaiokastritsa by way of the Ropas valley.

Ayioi Deka
Ai Gordis
Kynopiastes

At 7 km. from the town of Corfu there is a turn to the left for **Ayioi Deka**. The road twists and turns making its way up through dense olive groves to the beautiful village which is nestled on the side of the mountain with the same name. From here you can climb to the top of the mountain and admire the view in all directions. The church of the Pantokrator is located here and, further west, the church of the Profitis Ilias. The Metrological Station stands at the peak and is visible from almost all sides of the island.

After the turn for Agioi Deka, a turn to the right comes out at **Kynopiastes** (Bogies), the beauti-

The large beach of Ai Gordis, with the impressive rocks on the north side shaped by the sea into naturally-formed works of art. On the south edge of the beach is the famous Ortholithi, an imposing rock in the sea, the 'marker' of Ai Gordis.

ful white village with the strange name, known for its traditional tavernas with Corfiot music. The houses are interesting being examples of traditional Corfiot architecture.

You soon ascend high above the **beach of Ai Gordis** one of the beautiful sand beaches that have rightly made the west coast of Corfu famous. Ai Gordis is one of the most popular sandy beaches of Corfu. It took its name from the church of Agios Gordios (Saint Gordios), built almost on the waves as the centre of the beach. This is an idyllic site. The blue sea and the golden sand complement each other and form a single unit with the verdant landscape and the grey rocks.

Olive Museum

The olive tree is the characteristic flora of the Corfu earth. At Kynopiastes you can visit the Olive Museum, housed in a fully renovated century-old olive press. The Paipetis olive press was one of a thousand such that operated with the traditional method on the island until the 1970s. In the Museum you can admire a rich collection of tools for olive gathering and for oil extraction, which were used by the olive oil producers of Corfu. There are also photographs of rural life from the early 20th century.

Open from 18:00
(summer months)
Tel. 26610 49301-2

info

AI GORDIS
Location: The beach can be reached by car or by bus from Corfu town.
Type: Sandy beach with shallow waters that extends throughout the length of the gulf.
Services: Many large hotels, rented rooms, shops, and restaurants and bars for your evening's entertainment.
Activities: You can take boat trips and discover the other beaches. From the peak of the mountain, at a height of 370 metres, those who enjoy paragliding can practice their sport and fly down to the beach. To reach the take-off point climb up the mountain from the beach and continue until you pass Kato Garouna Square. Ai Gordis is an excellent destination for nature-lovers, who can enjoy endless walks in the verdant mountain.

Sinarades
Pelekas

Sinarades is a large farming village with a narrow, winding main street (12.5 km. from the town of Corfu). Sinarades is a large, well-preserved village with houses dating to the Byzantine and Venetian periods. Its 17th-century belfry is of great interest and, a little further down in a lane, is the old wood-fired kiln where traditional bread is made. The particular characteristics of the local architecture are the curved doors on the lower floor, the *volta* (porticos), the cornices on the roofs, the external doors with attractive relief designs on the marble, the external stone stairways that end in *verandas* (bonzzo), green window leaves and chimneys with curved walls. As soon as you enter the village and before you reach the main square you will see on your right a lovely mansion which houses the **Mesi Historical and Folklore Museum**.

As you leave the village a turn to the left takes you to the imposing **rock of Aerostatos** which during the time of the pirates was called "Sentry" because from there an eye could be kept on the western coasts of the island. In this region there is a pine forest that stretches out over the beaches of **Dechoumenon, Mavros Ammos, Mavron Plakon** and **Gialiskario**.

You return to the main road and soon come to the picturesque **Pelekas**, roosting on the top of its hill. The road passes through a pleasant, open agricultural area as if it were a continuation of the Ropas valley. Pelekas is certainly one of the most beautiful villages on the island. The fact that it is near so many fine beaches means that it now contains a fair number of tourist facilities but there are still quiet lanes for one to stroll through. The houses are painted in an amazing variety of colors.

The road branches in Pelekas the right part leading to the top of the hill (270 m.) above the village one point on the island that no visitor should miss. Generally speaking the west coast of Greece has superb sunsets but the west coast of Corfu is the best known place of all. And this is the classical place for one to watch the sun sink in to the purple water of the Ionian sea. This place achieved its status by the regular visits of Kaiser William II who came here for the same purpose This is why this place is called **"The Kaiser's throne"**.

Since the hill of Pelakas looms over a rather flat area of the island- the Ropas plain - one can see for a great distance in all directions and get an idea of the geographical, layout of the central part of Corfu, called "Mesi" which means middle).

info

At Pelekas you can enjoy a different type of holiday, with walks in the mountains and forests even just a few kilometres from the beach. In the surrounding area you can go horse riding or play golf. Don't miss the panoramic 360-degree view with the unique sunset.

Mesi Historical and Folklore Museum

This small Museum in the village of Sinarades opened in 1982 and is housed within a beautiful mansion. On the first floor of the building there is a dining room, kitchen and a small bedroom adorned with furniture and vessels of the period. Another section of the Museum, on the second floor, is dedicated to objects of daily use, such as vessels, musical instruments, pottery, clothes and fishing and farming equipment. There is also an office with various books and a collection of ancient documents that was donated to the Museum.

Daily (except Sundays) 9:00-14:00.
http://cmm.corfuculture.gr

Pelekas village, with the wonderful sunset over the Ionian Sea.

The beach of Kontogialos near Pelekas.

Palaiokastritsa with its two bays, Alipas bay and Agios Spyridon bay. Palaiokastritsa Monastery can be seen atop the front rock.

Glyfada
Kontoyialos

The road that passes through Pelekas divides. The left part winds its way down through olive groves to **Glyfada**, another enormous sand beach which has clear, shallow waters and recently has developed into an important tourist center

South of Glyfada is the highly frequented beach of **Kontoyialos** which you can reach by the road that goes through Pelekas.

info

GLYFADA
Type: Beach with very fine sands and shallow waters, suitable for children.
Services: Sun umbrellas and recliners for hire, showers and changing rooms. Plenty of restaurants and bars along the beach.
Activities: the Greek Beach Valley Competition is held here and there are opportunities for various water sports.

Above: Glyfada, one of the most beautiful beaches of Corfu and over a mile long.
Below: The beach at Gualiskara near Pelekas.

Aqualand

www.aqualand-corfu.com
Aqualand Water Park (before Agios Ioannis village) is one of the most impressive and largest water parks in Europe, covering an area of 75,000 square metres. Inside the Park you will find a large variety of water slides, water games and facilities. The Park has lifeguards and the pool water is changed daily. Special services are available for people with special needs. There are also sun recliners and umbrellas, training areas, restaurants, a small supermarket and a bar where you can enjoy your drink and many other comforts.
Opening hours: May-June: 10:00-18:00, July-August: 10:00-19:00, September-October: 10:00-18:00.

Ermones
Myrtiotissa monastery

The road that descends to Glyfada forks after Peleka and its right branch leads to **Ermones** and a beach with cold waters and precipitous rocks. Archaeological field studies have found traces of a Bronze Age settlement here. In the middle of this road a dirt road leads to the isolated **beach of Myrtidiotissa**, the only nudist beach on the island and perfect for snorkelling fans. Here there is also a 14th-century **monastery** dedicated to the Panagia. At Ermones there is a spring with running water where, according to tradition, Odysseus may have met Nausicaa for the first time.

The Ropas Valley

Returning to the junction below Pelekas you continue on following the sign that points to the town of Corfu. On your left you find the road that comes from Palaiokastritsa through the Ropas valley, one of the most beautiful and fertile areas of the island where the aristocracy had enormous estates in bygone days. But one can also take a secondary road along the west side of the valley and explore the small agricultural communities such as **Kanakades**, **Marmaro** and the larger **Iannades**. After crossing a bridge you find a secondary road that leads to **Kobitsi**. This is a very small village yet with three excellent examples of Corfiot mansions. For those not in a hurry, this is a delightful excursion that rejoins the central road a little further down. After the village of Alepou we enter Corfu town. For those who are not in a hurry this is pleasant detour and you can return to the main route shortly afterward. After the village of Alepou you again enter the town of Corfu.

info

ERMONES
Type: Beach with fine sands and pebbles.
Services: Sun umbrellas and recliners for hire, showers and changing rooms. Plenty of restaurants and bars along the beach.
Activities: Water bicycles for hire. There is an excellent scuba diving centre on the beach, which lies only one kilometre from the island's golf course.

Route Three

Potamos Salt Marshes, Kontokali, **Gouvia, Dasia,** Korakiana, Ypsos, **Pantokrator Mountain and Monastery,** Agios Markos, Spartylas, Strinillas, Petaleia, Barbati, Nisaki, Kalami, **Kouloura,** Agios Stephanos Sinion, Kassiopi, Peritheia, Antinioti Lagoon, **Acharavi**

Introduction   The northeast section of Corfu has been perhaps less influenced by the pas-sage of ti-me and tourism that has come to dominate the eastern shores of the islands the last few decades. Episkepsi, Spartillas, Strinillas, Petaleia and all the mountain villages in the shelter of Mt. Pantokratoras, so massive and imposing are like those on mainland Greece, nestled in their dense green vegetation. With their strong stone houses, the flocks of the shepherds and their open ranges in the mountains, they appear to be more a part of the wild mountains of Epirus which Corfu split apart from millions of years ago. Here the inhabitants life is ruled by the peace and quiet of nature as if nothing had changed after all the centuries of one conqueror succeeding another. Just as in former times, their occupations, traditions and customs have lent them a calm and sweet character. Further up the monastery of the Pantokrator looks down on the area with tranquillity and wisdom from high on its mountain and as if it too was guiding the inhabitants through a life of Byzantine austerity. Lower down the scene abruptly changes. On the northern shores where ancient Cassiopeia once flourished, a large harbor in antiquity that was destroyed by the Romans, pirates and invaders from the north, today there has been rapid tourist development making the place into an important seaside resort. The area has some of the most beautiful beaches on the island not only beautiful but unique which are there for anyone who comes in search of them opposite the mountains of the Balkans which stand out so clearly on the horizon. Monuments of the ruined castle at Cassiopeia will engrave on the visitor's memory images that will seem to emerge from the very waters of the Ionian sea.

The little church of Ypapanti at Gouvia and Lake Akolis near Agios Stephanos Sinion.

Potamos Salt Marshes
Kontokali
Gouvia

Leaving the town you follow the north coast road "Ethniki Palaiokastritsas". At the 4th km. you reach **Alykes Potamou.** Today little remains of the old salt mining activities aside from a ruined building of the 16th century, where salt was stored.

This is an important wetlands area. The village of **Potamos** is a traditional one with its "voltes" (Vaults). The area is fertile because of the river that passes through it and in times past it was a very rich village. The region's name comes from the river (potamos) that runs through it, the most splendid river on Corfu with the greatest volume of water.

After Alykes you will arrive at **Kontokali** and then **Gouvia**, 8 km. This is an old fishing village built on the bay of Gouvia. To your right is the little **island of Lazzareto** which was once the quarantine station for the entire island. You follow the **Bay of Gouvia** for some distance which has a full array of hotels, camping facilities, restaurants and sea sports and marinas are also available.

At this point are the ruins of the old Venetian Naval Station. One version holds that the village's name comes from the govioi, as the gobius fish is called here. This was a fishing village in the past, which specialised in this type of fishing. Gouvia beach is one of the most popular beaches of Corfu.

info

GOUVIA

Location: The beach can be reached by car or by bus from Corfu town.
Type: Small, pebbly beach.
Services: Sun umbrellas and recliners for hire. There are many large hotels, shops, and restaurants and bars for your evening's entertainment. Restaurants and bars also in the village behind the beach.
Activities: Water sports and boat trips.

The ruins of the Venetian naval station, the Arsenal, where the galleys of the Venetian fleet were repaired. Today only large sections of the walls, the columns and arches of the vaults survive, whilst the roof is completely missing.

Below: The marina at Gouvia gulf, used for the mooring of at least 900 tourist and other boats.

The small church of the Hypapantis on the north edge of Gouvia bay, on Kommenos peninsular, is built on a small island that is connected to the dry land by a footpath. The view from here is wonderful as you can see the whole of the gulf, the old town and the coast of south Albania. It is a simple structure of no historical importance, yet set within an amazing environment especially during sunset.

Lazareto

The islet of Lazareto is uninhabited. It is located opposite the region of Kontokali-Gouvia and is a place of particular natural beauty with dense and varied vegetation and of especial historical value. There are two views on the origin of its name. According to the first it took its name from the church that was dedicated to the Panagia Nazaret (La Nazaret, as it is believed the Venetians called her). The ruins of the church are still visible. The second view attributes the name to the quarantine (*lazaretto*) that existed on the island during the Venetian period. During the Second World War the islet was used as concentration camp for captives from the National Resistance. After liberation and until 1962 it was the place of execution for approximately 200 political prisoners. The execution wall still survives today, being none other than the surviving wall of the now ruined church of the Panagia Nazaret. The islet is today a site of memory for the executed and various organisations hold commemorations on and pilgrimages to the islet every year.

Dasia
Kato and Ano Korakiana
Ypsos

info

DASIA

Type: Long and narrow beach with pebbles and sand.
Services: Sun umbrellas and recliners for hire. There are many hotels, shops, restaurants with international cuisine and traditional tavernas as well as bars for your evening's entertainment.
Activities: Water sports, boat trips, horse riding and golf.
Features: The sea along this point of the coast is very calm and almost flat. From the beach you can admire the mountains of Albania and its hinterland.

At Tzabros (9.5 km.) you turn right for Kassiopi leaving the road to Palaiokastritsa. The road passes through the same Cape Kommenos. This area, which is called **Dasia**, has been heavily developed for tourism with large hotels and a full range of facilities.

On your left you will pass the road that leads to **Kato Korakiana** a little further from the coast. There is an annex of the National Gallery here. It is housed in two auxiliary buildings, the Kastellino and the Kastelleto, which belonged to the historic Kastello hotel. Leading European figures were guests at the hotel, including the Austro-Hungarian Emperor Franz Joseph, Kaiser Wilhelm, the King of Italy Victor Emmanuel, George I of Greece and George II of Greece, who even chose this tower as his permanent place of residence from 1936 until 1939. The Castellino and Castelleto buildings were renovated in1992. As of 1994 many temporary exhibitions have taken place. The works of important 19th and 20th century artists are part of the permanent exhibition.

As you continue on the road you will arrive at **Ano Korakiana.** It is a traditional, conserved village with a large number of churches both within and around it. One of the most important churches is the 16th-century church of Agios Athanasios. There is a pottery workshop that you can visit, in the district of Felekas. The inhabitants are art lovers, as can be seen in the painting exhibition that

Left: Kastello, a Gothic villa formerly owned by the Italian baron Luca Mimbelli. Built by Italian engineers according to the design of the medieval tower that had formerly stood on this spot.
Right: Wall painting in the church of Agios Athanasios at Ano Korakiana.

is held here every year during the first tehn days of August. Other sites in the village are the villa of the writer Iakovo Polylas and the neoclassical Elementary School built in 1932, which now houses a small folklore collection.

You come back close to the sea at **Ypsos** (14 km.) a resort area with a large beach. This area is particularly popular during the summer and is one of the most developed on Corfu with facilities for camping and sea sports. Part of its charm is the mass of Mt. Pantokratoras rising up in the background from amid the olive groves that cover its lower slopes.

Merlin Estate: Located in Dasia, it was the estate of the British gardener Merlin, who experimented and created the Merlin variety of oranges. He brought the kumquat to Greece from Japan, the fruit which has become a trademark of the island.

Ypsos, one of the most developed regions of Corfu. A sandy beach with very clean waters that does not suddenly become deep. Great for water sports and with its own scuba diving centre. Ypsos can also satisfy all one might want from its nightlife.

Pantokrator Mountain and Monastery

In a distance 12. 5 km along the main excursion you turn right on a road which after 4.5 km. leads to the top of **Mt. Pantokratoras** (960 m.). As you go up you see the small plots of land that have been cultivated among the barren rocks. The top of the mountain know to the British as Mount San Salvatore, gives one an incredible view when the atmosphere is clear. The entire island spreads out before you and Paxoi and Lefkada to the south and Albania to the east. It is said that on especially clear days even Italy can be seen. In the north you can see the peak of the same name (914 m), the Monastery and the antennas.

The **Pantokratoras monastery** built on top of the mountain was built on the site of another monastery in 1347 during the time of the Angevins and was destroyed at the beginning of the 16th century. The monastery one sees today is from the 19th century. During the first week in August pilgrims from all Corfu come to celebrate the monastery's feast-day. The feast day of the Pantokrator is held on 6August, the island's largest with a pilgrimage lasting for six days (1-6 August). The inhabitants of the surrounding villages, armed with candles and torches, climb up the footpaths in the evening.

On Mount Pantokrator you must visit the village of Nymphes at an altitude of 200 metres, known in antiquity as Neraidochori. Its name is said to have come from the nymphs who bathed in its waterfalls. Visit Estavromenos church in the village, unique for its Byzantine style, the Monastery of the Metamorphosis Askitario and Agia Triada at Klimatia.

Mount Pantokrator, 911 metres high, is the island's tallest point. Weather permitting, you can see Paxoi to the south of Corfu and the Diapontia Islands in the north.

At the end of the bay and beyond the settlement of **Pyrgi** the road begins to climb steeply and you pass the turn-off for Ayios Markos (2 km.) a pretty village with an exceptional view toward Ypsos and a heavily forested area in the background. The village's great authenticity is truly impressive and it is protected not simply for its scattered monuments but for the whole complex. Outside its own particular beauties-Italian cafes with covered balconies in the back so that one has a better chance to enjoy the view. Near Ayios Markos there are two exceptional churches: the Pantokrator with superbly preserved wall paintings from 1576 and Ayios Merkourios which is dated to the 11th century and which after the church of the Saints Jason and Sosipatros in the town is the most important Byzantine monument on the island. It survived the harsh test of around 1000 years. Located in the region of Agios Markos, it is hidden within an olive grove on a privately-owned estate. A dedicatory inscription indicates that it was built in 1075. The two conches in the sanctuary are idiosyncratic. There is an annex that is larger than the church in south wall. Inside are rich yet worn wall paintings of various periods. The oldest are contemporaneous with the construction of the church, whilst the latest date to the second half of the 14th or early 15th century.

Agios Markos

info

The Club Méditerranée (Club Med) was established in the region of Agios Markos over forty years ago by the French entrepreneur Gérard Blitz. Open until recently, this was the first tourism facility of Corfu and one of the first in Greece.

Wall painting in the church of Agios Merkurios at Agios Markos.

Laskaris Mansion

On the slopes of Mount Agios Markos, with a view over the sea, there stands a building constructed in 1617 and covering a space of 1400 square metres. It is filled with a pervading atmosphere of the centuries and the magic of past times. The building was the mansion of the Laskaris family, and a faithful copy of a house in Mystras, from where the first residents came. It is a unique house that has amazingly been able to maintain its identity and its functions unchanged over the centuries. Inside, stone plays the leading role, with the arches and elegant wooden ceilings personifying the luxury. A rich collection of rare furniture adorns all the rooms and the family's personal possessions each carry their own story. The kitchen is full of cooking equipment from an earlier era, such as the wood-fired oven, the icemakers and the coffee grinder. There are also other spaces where hanging from the walls we find all the agricultural tools of Corfu as well as various household items such as the distaff, the flax container and others whose use has been forgotten over time. A surprise awaits us in the cellar of the farmhouse, where the owner had left the olive oil stores untouched, with barrels, pictures and old tools. The oldest item in the house was a Byzantine plate that was found buried two metres under the ground.

Spartyla
Strinillas
Petaleia

16 km. along the man road a turn to the left takes you to Spartillas and **Episkepsi**, villages built on the slopes of Mt. Pantokrator. This turn is the beginning of a brief but spectacular tour. First of all it gives you the chance to reach the top of the highest mountain in Corfu and to enjoy a view of the island that few visitors have had the chance to enjoy. Here is where one can truly delight in the grandeur of its mountains and the wild beauty in which its mountain villages are nestled.

After 6 km. you enter the medieval village of **Spartillas** with its narrow alleyways and its balconies jutting out over the steep mountain slope. The area around Spartillas is the lowest on M. Pantokrator (400 m.) and is rich in spring water. Neolithic and Bronze Age structures and artefacts have been found in the region of Spartyla. The following churches in Spartyla are worth visiting: Koimisis tis Theotokou, where fairs are also held; Agios Arsenios at the edge of the steep slope of Pantokratoras;, considered the original church of Spartyla; and the parish church of Agios Spyridon.

Just before Sgourades there is a turn right to **Strinillas** and Pantokratoras. From there the road winds its way upward like a snake through a mountainous landscape that becomes more and more barren with a view of the northern and the southern part of the island. The village is famous for its good wine, which you can sample in the picturesque tavernas.

Strinillas, as well as the neighboring vilage of **Petaleia** occupy a small plateau at a height of 700 m. Once cereals and grapes were grown in these areas. Animal husbandry was also very important and there were large herds of sheep and goats. The hillsides cut in relief allowed the villages to be irrigated to height of 600 m. The houses look like cubes and are built of great stone blocks and are really architectural complexes. This is the typical welcoming one finds in these limestone mountains. Just beyond the beautiful square with it's shady trees you can admire the view of the north side of the mountain.

Charming lane with a panoramic view over Spartyla.

Returning to the main road, you continue your excursion along the sea. You then reach the top of the Hill which has a very fine view of the sand beach of **Barbati**. As with most of the main beaches the road does not go directly along the sea. But there are many dirt tracks and paths that wind their way down to the sea through the trees.

Barbati has a beautiful beach with sand and white pebbles, filled with small gulfs and crystal-clear waters. The village has both mountain and sea on the same spot.

From here to Kassiopi there are some superb views in both directions along the coast. Passing through the small seaside settlement of **Glyfa** and entering the area of **Nisaki** (23 km.) which is made up of the settlements of Kentromas, Kavalairna, Loustri and Yiamris, and with its well-known fish tavernas. One could literally spend days exploring this piece of the coastline. From Yimaris one has a truly magnificent view all the way down to Kalami.

Barbati
Nisaki

info

All the beaches in this area have sun recliners and umbrellas for hire and there are also many options for water sports and scuba diving.

Small photograph, right: Picturesque coasts with tourism facilities (Nisaki) and sandy gulfs (Kalami) can be found in the channel, known as Kanali, which divides the island from the mainland.

Blue and green attempt to mix at Barbati. This is one of the many award-winning beaches of Corfu, with a Blue Flag for its clean waters.

Kalami
Kouloura
Agios Stephanos Sinion

At the 25th km. you take the road to the right for Kalami and Kouloura. After a short distance the road divides and the right part goes to **Kalami** where it ends. The beach runs along the whole length of the village and is the favoured destination for all those seeking quiet, clear waters and a beautiful panorama to gaze at. When swimming, explore the section of the coast to the left of the beach where there is another small bay.

The other part goes left to **Kouloura** a very pretty little fishing harbor. It owes its name ("kouloura" means ring-shape) to the shape of its harbor. The remains of a fortified Venetian residence can still be found there. After Kouloura a turn to the right takes you to **Ayios Stephanos Sinion** (3 km.) Half way along travelling through olive groves there suddenly appears before you a view of the small bay of Ayios Stephanos with its cozy beach and beautiful houses. Here the distance between Greece and Albania is only 2 km.

Opposite page:
Above: Kalami, with the sandy bay.
Centre: Agios Stephanos Sinion.
Below: Lake Akoli, near Agios Stephanos Sinion.

Kerasia

Kerasia is considered one of the island's most beautiful beaches, with a clear and clean sea, white pebbles and the colour of the sea that ranges from emerald green to dark blue. Kerasia beach stretches out a little before Kassiopi, near to Agios Stephanos and there are few houses and even fewer tavernas for you to dine at along the coast. You can also admire the wild coasts between Greece and Albania, which lie only a few kilometres distant. At Kerasia you can only rent canoes or sea cycles.

Kouloura: The small lake took its name from its circular (*kouloura*) shape, whilst the restored Venetian house on its edge makes the landscape particularly charming.

Kassiopi

The picturesque market town of Kassiopi (36 km.) lies on exactly the same site it did in antiquity. During the Roman period Kassiopi was a flourishing town because of its geographical position, right on a sea lane. In 48 B.C, Cicero spent six days in Kassiopi. Nero was another Roman visitor to Kassiopi who went there during one of his processions through Greece. With an enormous entourage of actors and singers he arrived there in 67 B.C. and danced before the altar of Cassios Zeus. This shrine dedicated to Zeus was famous in antiquity and is probably the site on which the **church to the Panayia Kassiopissa** (Virgin Mary of Kassiopi) is found today. This church was also one of the most venerated religious sites on the island and the ships that went through the straits there always saluted it with cannonades. The building that you see today is dated to the 16th century with wall paintings from the 17th century. The icon of the Panagia was painted by Poulakis, the great icon painter of the Cretan school, and is believed to be miracle-working

The **Castle of Kassiopi** is on a hill above two small coves which were the harbors of the medieval town and occupies a site that has been fortified since antiquity. When the Venetians decided to take control of Corfu, the residents of Kassiopi decided to resist and fortifying themselves in their castle resisted these "rabid" attacks. When in the end the Venetians managed to capture the town as a punishment they laid the town waste leaving Kassiopi nearly uninhabitable. The consequence of this was that during every hostile raid Kassiopi stripped of its defenses, was naturally the first target. In the end its inhabitants were forced to move to other parts of the island.

Kassiopi is an excellent base for one to begin his exploration of the north side of the island.

info

KASSIOPI

Type: The first large beach with pebbles is located on the left of the island. The smaller beach behind the Cape has more character.

Services: Sun umbrellas and recliners for hire on both beaches. There are many rented rooms, shops, restaurants and bars for your evening's entertainment.

Activities: Water sports, boat trips, horse riding and cycling. There is a scuba diving centre at Kassiopi.

Peritheia
Antinioti
Lagoon

You set off from Kassiopi and head toward Roda. About six kilometers along the way and just before you turn for the salt lake there is a road on your left with the sign **Peritheia**. It is worth while for one to take this short excursion (14 km.) both for the beauty of the mountain landscape and to get a taste of how different the architecture and the atmosphere of the mountain villages of Corfu is. Peritheia is built quite high up on the sides of Pantokratoras. The natural landscape throughout the valley is astonishingly beautiful: grass, trees and flowers of all colours form the background in which stand, some in ruins but some also renovated, the village houses. All are built in the traditional Corfiot architectural style. Most have an external stone staircase that leads to the first floor through a balcony with columns that in the Corfiot dialect

Mansion in Peritheia.

Fishermen still fish at Kassiopi lake, which has the atmosphere and simplicity characteristic of traditional Greek culture.

Kassiopi with its castle and small lake. The ruined castle is dated to the Angevin period. Paradoxically, the existence of the castle also brought the end of mediaeval Kassiopi.

Agios Spyridon bay.

are called bozzes. Beneath the bozzes is the volta (portico) whilst on the ground floor is the katoi, which was used to store wine and oil. There are at least seven churches in the village and some believe that the village name comes from peri and theia, i.e. from the fact that the village is close to these dedications to God.

Immediately after the turn-off for Peritheia you leave the main road once more and this time go right to **Ayios Spyridonas** which leads to a new group of tourist facilities and then a beach.

The **Antinioti Salt Lake** is directly on your left. The area is of especial interest for nature-lovers. There is an enormous variety of wild flowers and a station for migratory birds not counting all the water fowl that live there throughout the year (see page 12, nature).

Acharavi

The main road continues on to the southwest and at the 10th km. (from Kassiopi) arrives at **Acharavi** which is a highly developed tourist resort on one of the finest sand beaches on the north side of the island. You leave Acharavi and follow the road to Episkepsi and **Ayios Panteleimonas.** The road is narrow and hard to drive on and one should be very cautious but whomever chooses to drive along it is richly rewarded with an amazing view of all north Corfu.

Episkepsi (6 km. from the main road) is a large and friendly village, untouched until now by tourism which gives you a true picture of the daily life of most Corfiots. After Episkepsi the road continues on to the village of **Sgourades** and a bit further down joins the road to Pantokratora. It is considered one of the oldest on Corfu. The houses are well built and the mansions grand. In the square of Agios Vasilios the custom of the 'Dance of the Priests' is held on Cheese Sunday.

From Acharavi you can also visit **Kalamaki, Avlaki and Almyros beaches.** Kalamaki has sands and shallow waters and you can hire sea cycles. Avlaki has white pebbles and is fully equipped with beach facilities, with water sports and a yachting school. Almyros lies two kilometres from Acharavi and has a number of sand dunes. It is known for its shallow waters and is an ideal place for children to play on the golden sands.

Almyros beach.

The beautiful sandy beach of Acharavi on the slopes of Mt. Pantokratoras.

info
ACHARAVI
Type: Large beach with pebbles and sand.
Services: Sun umbrellas and recliners can be hired at certain points and there are also showers. Some restaurants and bars can be found along the beach although most are in the village.
Activities: Water sports, boat trips and scuba diving. There is a water park and pitches for beach volley and basketball.
Features: The waters are shallow for several metres in, making this a safe beach for children.

Acharavi Folk Museum
museum-acharavi.webs.com
The Museum is located opposite the archaeological site of the Roman baths of Acharavi. The

exhibits have a particular cultural, folklore and historical interest as some date to even before 1700. In the Museum you will be able to see: banknotes and coins from the period of the Ionian state until 2001; local female costumes from 1800; stone objects, vessels, lamp lighters; a sun clock; a traditional olive press; presses and other agricultural tools; an exhibit on wine and *tsipouro* spirit production; a watermill; witchcraft and other tools; looms, distaffs, spinning wheels, handicrafts; children's toys; and, a rich collection of photographs and old books and documents from 1862.

Route Four

Roda, Agios Georgios Pagon, Arillas, **Sidari,
Peroulades**, Agios Stephanos Avlioton

Introduction
The section of the island of Corfu that lies directly opposite Italy and at the entrance to the Adriatic Sea is one of the most beautiful places in all the Ionian islands. Since ancient times the area has been known for its development, mainly in its northern part as can be seen from the ruins in the area of Roda. The medieval fortifications and towers lying in ruins amid the shrubbery or clinging to the sides of cliffs still tell us something of the difficult times the island went through with the successive waves of invaders. The quaint villages in the interior, however, far from the tourist centers, still retain something of the true flavor of Corfu, which is always friendly and alive with music and good spirits.

The famous Canal d'Amour at Sidari is an opening within the rock in the sea, a tunnel. Tradition holds that someone once swam through this channel to the other side in order to meet the love of his life. The beach has small bays and caves scattered along it. The sandstone has been weathered by the water and the wind, forming impressive shapes that you might think had been carved by an eccentric artist. The Canal of Love at Sidari is one of a series of rock formations that stretch out into the sea, creating some little gulfs that you can reach along small paths and steps, a canal filled with crystal-clear waters. A swim with mask and flippers is highly recommended, so that you can discover the caves hidden along the channel.

The beaches in the area have a unique kind of beauty. Today, Ayios Georgios ton Pagon and Arillas have made rapid strides in tourist development using Corfiot hospitality and beauty as their main weapons. These elements have all come together at Sidari, one of the most important summer resorts not only on the island but in all the Ionian Islands. Both the famed Canal d'Amour and the vegetation that runs riot in the area are its main attractions. There are also many excursions that leave from its harbor for the Diapontia islands these quiet and beautiful isles which set the western border of Greece.

Setting off from the crossroads at the 8th kilometer at Yuatroi you will soon pass through the village on **Skriperos** and then you begin to climb leaving behind you, on your left, the road to Palaiokastritsa. The uphill road ends at **Perasma of Troumbetas** where there is a view of the whole northwest side of the island. If you turn left on the road to the villages of **Aleimmatades** and **Vistona** you will be recompensed by a superb view in all directions.

Opposite page:
Views of magical Sidari
and the Canal d'Amour.

Roda Descending from the level area of the northwest side of the island you reach a junction, the right part of which leads to the villages of Cherepisko-poi Ayioi Douloi, Xanthates, Platanos and Afra before arriving at Roda and Acharavi. This entire area, stretching out behind the mass of Mt. Pantokratoras is of particular archaeological and historical interest. The area is full of finds from the ancient Greek and Roman periods (especially the ruins of the 5th-century BC Doric temple of Apollo). Many of these, on display at the Archaeological Museum of Corfu, have been saved from the ruins of a medieval tower.

Roda (37 km.) was a farming community but now because of its beautiful sandy beach - nearly 8 km. long - which goes all the way down to Acharavi, it has developed into a modern tourist center.

info

RODA
Type: Both beaches have solid sands.
Services: Sun umbrellas and recliners for hire. Restaurants and bars along the beach as well as in the village. Roda has a number of options for accommodation and shopping.
Activities: Boat trips.
Features: The sea becomes deep quite suddenly.

On the road to Roda you will encounter **Astrakeri** beach. The *astrakeri* in the local Corfiot dialect is the place that is covered with *astrakes*, coastal schrubs. This is an ideal family beach and the shallow waters and boundless sands are great for children. The beach has some organised facilities and swimmers can easily find sun umbrellas and recliners for hire and there are also a few tavernas. There is a long mole where the fishermen tie their boats, perfect for a stroll.

Karousades

The region of Karousades is one of the sites of special natural beauty in Greece and is included in the Greek nature database. It is a charming traditional village with few architectural changes having been made to the buildings, surrounded by olive groves and cypress trees and with a great view from many spots. The village was settled in 20 BC by the Karysoi, Pontian refugees. It was an administrative centre during the Byzantine Empire, when it flourished economically. The Theotokis family settled here in 1453, an important historic family with a leading role in the island's economic and cultural life. Their grand mansion, built in 1500, survives today.

The other part of the junction with the side that says "Pros Sidari" which goes above a village with a rather mysterious Greek name **Kastelelanoi Gyrou** (The Castellan of Gyrou) and then again divides at the village of Arkadades. The left branch goes to the village of **Pagoi** and ends at the coastline, at **Ayios Georgios ton Pagon** ("St. George of the Ice"). Archaeological finds from Pagi village indicate that the region has been inhabited since the Roman period. The building of the Venetian pantiera survives in a ruinous condition, with impressive architectural features (external entrance doors). There are also mansions from the late 18th and early 19th centuries.

Ai Giorgis Pagon is not only a fantastic beach for those seeking crystal-clear waters but its northwest wind makes it perfect for windsurfing, and the beach is popular with water sports enthusiasts.

Long, tall olive trees and green-brown cypresses frame the magical beach of Ai Giorgis Pagon. The beach is sandy and very long. All the needs of the demanding visitor are met, with accommodation, shops and water sports.

Arillas beach is famed for its shallow, crystal-clear waters, stunning sunset and fine golden sands that are perfect for families with small children. You can also go windsurfing and hire boats or use a taxi boat in order to visit the neighbouring islets.

Near Pagi beach you can visit **Prinylas**, a conserved settlement with lanes, houses and a mansion characteristic of the early 20th century.

The enchanting landscape of Ayios Georgios ton Pagon in nestled in the tranquil Corfiot landscape with its lofty olive trees, the somber green cypress trees and the steep coast of Arillas. One can make a tour of this small head lead from the sea all the way to **Afiona** a beautiful little harbor on the south and of the shallow **Bay of Arillas**. On a piece of dry land that separates the two bays there are the ruins of old walls and gates which bear witness to foreign occupation and the fortifications of past generations. The foundations of the walls are ancient, but the upper masonry is more recent and seems likely to date from around the time to Angelokastro.

The main road now passes through **Agros** where it again splits. The left part of the road, before reaching the sea, passes through villages that are still untouched by tourism and then reaches Arillas, north of Afiona where it also ends (39 km. from the town of Corfu).

Magical Peroulades.

Sidari
Peroulades
Agios Stephanos
Avlioton

info

PEROULADES: A traditional village with a rich architectural heritage from the Venetian period. You will find *volta* (porticoes), characteristic doors, old-fashioned greengrocers and the ruins of the house in which the poet Kalvos lived. A road from here leads you to the wonderful beach of Kavo Drasti.

Right page: The 'sculpture' of Corfu is to be found at Sidari, its most beautiful personification.

Below: The large beach of Agios Stephanos Avlioton. This huge, sandy beach has turqoise crystal-clear waters and the EU Blue Flag indicates that it is safe and perfect for families with small children, who will enjoy playing in the golden sands. Agios Stephanos offers its bathers all the necessary comforts, such as sun umbrellas and recliners, beach bars and small tavernas.

The other road at the junction at Agros goes nearly straight through the northwest areas of the island until it reaches **Sidari** (35 km.) an open bay on the west side of the north coast. It is an important resort with a beautiful sandy beach and every kind of facility a tourist might require. One of its most important beauties is the sandy channel through the sea which has come to be called **"Canal d'Amour"** (see page 144). Sidari is without a doubt the touristic center of this side of the island.

From Sidari one can also go to the shore of **Peroulades**, to **Avliotes**, a rather large village and to the settlement of **Ayios Stephanos** with its isolated headland and lighthouse. This settlement his too begun to experience some tourist development because it has a marvellous sand beach and a clean sea. The road from here continues on to Arillas and Afiona.

Longa is located near the village of Peroulades and its beach is one of the island's most magical. A long row of steps leads you down to the beach, with its fine sands and very clean and crystal-clear waters. Sunset is a perfect time to visit Longa as the sun is positioned right in front of the beach as it descends into the sea.

Another excursion that one can take from Sidari is to the **Diapontia islands** of **Marthaki, Othonoi** and **Erikousa** which are about 7 miles from the mainland (see p. 162). There are normally caiques that make trips to these sparsely inhabited little islands which are the true end of the Greek State to the west.

Taking the same road back four kilometers south to Livadi, after 5 km. the road to the east leads to **Karousades** where the old Theotokis mansion is located. The road goes on to Roda. From Roda you turn to the right and passing through the beautiful villages of **Sfakera, Xanthates, Ayioi Douloi and Chorepiskopoi** you arrive at the junction we mentioned above, just before Kastelanoi Gyros. This side of Corfu can also be reached of course from the road from Kassiopi. Agioi Douloi is a picturesque village with traditional Venetian houses and Byzantine origins.

info

SIDARI

Type: there are three main beaches. The first is long and sandy, very touristy. The second is the small and beautiful gulf located opposite with rocky formations. The third is the Canal d'Amour (Canal of Love).

Services: Sun umbrellas and recliners for hire. Restaurants and bars along the beach.

Activities: boat trips, sea cycles and canoes. There is a scuba diving centre and you can also enjoy other water sports.

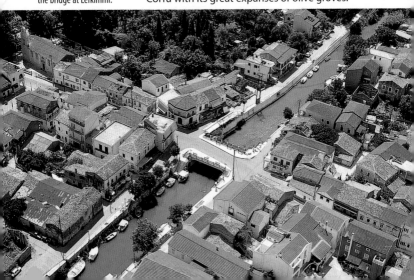

Route Five

Perama, Gastouri, Benitses, Moraitika, Mesongi, Chlomos, Agios Georgios Argyradon, Korission Lagoon, Argyrades, Marathias, Perivoli, Lefkimmi, Kavos, Arkoudilas, Spartera, Gardiki, Agios Matthaios

Introduction

This excursion covers the entire southern section of the island and that makes it the largest we have described. In south Corfu the morphology of the coastline, the landscape and the vegetation is completely different from that in the north. It is characterized by large sand beaches such as the largest on in the area of lake Koryssia which is 14 km. long with pines and sand dunes. The interior is rather flat (except for the central part) and it is a tranquil landscape. It is an incredibly lovely area which has rapidly developed the past few years. There are two roads to south Corfu. The one is the faster coast road which is being continually upgraded and on which you can reach Lefkimmi in less than one hour. The other road -much slower -goes through the hinterland along the "spine" of the island. In order to get on to this road one leaves the town and takes the road toward Ayioi Deka. Then the road winds its way uphill through beautiful landscapes and densely wooded areas before joining up once more with the coast road, at Vraganiotrika. We will be describing the coastal route. But at the same time it is worthwhile just wandering through the picturesque interior of south Corfu with its great expanses of olive groves.

In this part of Corfu, the greenery and the sands compete with each other.

Right page: View of Moraitika and, below, the bridge at Lefkimmi.

Perama

The bridge the Kaiser used to go to the beach from Achilleion.

Ascending from the town of Corfu and passing by the airport you then turn left for Perama and Benitses. **Perama**, practically hidden by its riotous vegetation which goes all the way down to the coves on the beautiful sand beaches is a fabulous country site very close to the town of Corfu (7 km.)

There is a spectacular view of Kanoni from here. From Perama you can go on foot uphill to Kanoni. Moving on toward Benitses following a lovely route along the coast you advance till you reach the **Kaiser's bridge** over which the royal entourage passed on its way to the Achilleio (see next chapter) having crossed the jetty on the other side of the town.

Panoramic view of Perama.

Gastouri
Benitses

Aside from the Achilleion you can visit **Gastouri**, which preserves the traditional Corfu architecture and way of life. Don't forget to buy bread from the wood-fired bakery located on a small road that comes off the central road. You should also visit the traditional hamlet of Agios Prokopios. The church of Agios Vasilios, found here from as early as 1511, is representative of the local architecture. Its paintings of saints are excellent examples of the local folk tradition. The olive tree of Ai Prokopis is the largest and oldest olive tree on the island, with a trunk circumference of 19 metres. On 8 July the village celebrates one of the oldest and most celebrated fairs on the island.

The clean beaches and the dense vegetationof Benitses always impresses visitors. Near this site by the sea are the sources of the hydragogeion of Corfu and the ruins of Roman spas with inlaid mosaic floors. According to one story the Homeric king Alkinoos had his "magical" garden here. The area is also a good one for walks far removed from heavy traffic.

info

There are several beaches near Benitses, all with both sand and pebbles. Various activities are available at the largest where you can also hire boats, whilst the smaller beaches are quieter. The crystal-clear waters become deep very suddenly. There are shops, restaurants, and accommodation available.

Most of the events and fairs at Benitses take place between 15 June and 15 August, where you can experience Corfiot traditions from up close. These include: the fair of St John the Torch Bearer with the fires on 22 June, and the large fair of Saint Marina on 16 and 17 July with the fires of St John. From Benitses you can visit **Koutsomaroula**, an idyllic little gulf perfect for swimming with trees running down to the beach and many shops, as well as the beach at **Loutrouvia**.

Staying on the coast road to the south and after the beautiful beach of **Ayios Ioannis Peristeron** (St. John of the Doves) you reach Moraitika.

Above: The beach of Agios Ioannis Peristeron with sand and pebbles and lots of water sports opportunities.
Below: Cosmopolitan Benitses. Excursions throughout the whole island are organised from its little port.

Corfu Shell Museum

The Corfu Shell Museum, is located in Benitses. Its exhibits include not only artefacts from the magical depths of the Mediterranean but also from tropical seas, such as the Indian and Pacific Oceans. There are over 10,000 wonderful and mysterious objects, such as: shells, marine fossils, sponges, coral reefs, salted fish, lobsters, sharks and shark jaws

Information:
Tel. 26610 72227 or 42900
www.corfushellmuseum.com
Open daily from
10 am – 9 pm.

Moraitika
Mesongi

Two small villages are located on both sides of the estuaries of the River Mesongi: **Moraitika** (18 km) and Mesongi. Moraitika is a spread out resort village with plenty of tourist facilities. The area itself has probably been inhabited since the Neolithic period. The panoramic view from the church of the Koimisis tis Theotokou at Moraitika is fantastic. In Moraitika there are the ruins of a Roman residence, a fountain and baths. The area betweeen Moraitika and Mesongi has a great deal of business in the summer.

Near **Mesongi**, higher up on the mountain is a small temple dated to the 3rd century B.C. Remnants of a Graeco-Roman building have been found at the mouth of the river. On the hill behind Mesongi is a church from the 16th century, with wall paintings and icons. Throughout the whole distance you will find beautiful beaches for swimming, with warm waters and good tourism services. Mesongi beach is divided by the River Mesongi at this point. **Boukaris** is a fishing village in a verdant setting, just like Mesongi. The visitor can enjoy extremely fresh sea delicacies and have a swim in the crystal-clear waters. Boukaris is especially recommended for families and those in search of peace and quiet.

info

MORAITIKA

The beach, with pebbles and sand, is equipped with facilities for water sports, scuba diving and boat trips to Lefkimmi gulf. Moraitika has many bars with live music and clubs open till late at night. Its shallow waters make it perfect for children.

Left: The beach of Moraitika.
Below: View from Mesongi.

Chlomos

Agios Georgios
Argyradon

Korission
Lagoon

After the junction for Mesongi the road turns south toward the interior of the island. Further down you will encouter the road from Ayioi Deka and turning left go to Lefkimmi. Immediately afterward there is a turn to the right for Ayios Matthaios which is the road you will return on. The are has a large oak forest and olive trees which go all the way up to the monastery of the Pantokrator.

At the 27th km, there is a turn left for **Chlomos** a picturesque village with old houses. This village lies near the top of a hill with a view to the south. The scattered ruins on the mountain slopes and the former existence of an altar to Apollo on the site of today's Taxiarches church prove that this area was inhabited even before the Early Christian period.

After one kilometer there is a crossroads to the right which leads to the **beach at Ayios Georgios.** Ayios Georgios is a large sand beach, more than three kilometers long which to the north goes all the way to the **Salt Lake of Koryssia** (see page 12 nature). This salt lake cover an area of 11,000 stremmata (roughtly 3,000 acres) full of sand-dunes and cedars and is separated from the sea by a strip of sand. A stone axe was found around the lake, indicating human activity in this region from the Lower Neolithic period (100,000 BC).

The beach of Agios Georgios Argyradon is wide and sandy with shallow waters that are safe for children. It has sun recliners and umbrellas and has been awarded the Blue Flag for cleanliness. The region has a variety of tavernas, cafes and hotels.

Argyrades
Marathias
Perivoli

Marta, a huge beach at Perivoli with the typical features of the southern beaches: fine sands and shallow waters.

Another base for making interesting excursions into the island is the village of **Argyrades** (30.5 km.). The lanes, *volta* (arched porticoes) and house architecture are very reminiscent of the Venetian period. The road that goes to the left from the crossroads in the center of the village leads to a small outcropping with various smaller settlements. The picturesque little port of **Petriti** to the south is set in a beautiful landscape with fishing tavernas, a view towards Epirus and a rich history.

Marathias (34 km.) is the narrowest point of the island where Corfu is less than 6.5 km wide. Dirt roads branch off both left and right of the road going to various beaches and since the distances are short one can choose whatever attracts him.

Further south is **Perivoli** a farming village with a beautiful beach, at **Kalyviotis**. Perivoli is an old, traditional village. The traditional architecture of its houses is characteristic and its churches are beautiful, especially Agion Saranta and the celebrated Pantokrator, set in a charming verdant environment. Perivoli also has an excellent beach at **Marta**, three km from the village. Another beach worth visiting is at the village of **Vitalades** (after Perivoli). This beach is relatively unknown to tourists and is safely secluded for those who wish to enjoy their swim without any hustle and bustle.

Lefkimmi
Salt Marshes

The salt marshes are located at cape Lefkimmi, which sailors know well for its lighthouse. This area was for many years used for salt mining and so is not particularly accessible as a beach or usable for holidaymakers. In the past few years salt mining has ceased and the area has thus been able to show its beauty and its wonderful natural landscape. Renovation has also been carried out on its buildings and facilities and the whole area has been upgraded. Large sandy beaches with crystal-clear waters await you during the Corfu summer.

Lefkimmi

The largest market town on the south side of the island is Lefkimmi (41 km.). It is one of the most picturesque areas in the whole Prefecture as its image has remained virtually untouched over the centuries: narrow lanes, tall houses, little squares, churches and coffeehouses are all reminders of past eras. There are a large number of vineyards and it is renowned for its wine.

It consists of five villages (**Riglades, Anaplades, Ayioi Theodori, Potami** and **Melikia**) and that is why the area is called the "Five-Villages". Riglades is the first village in Lefkimmi, with traditional mansions and folk architecture. The Philharmonic Orchestra holds a popular concert every 15 August, which you must not miss. The main thing to see there is the small channel that passes through the center of the town with a small bridge and trees that shade it. A walk through the lanes of Lefkimmi with its small shops and workshops, gives the visitor some idea of just how people make their living in these agricultural and commercial communities.

As you enter Lefkimmi there is a turn with a sign that says "**Petridis Beach**" which leads to some salt marshes. This area in the southern part of the sland is worth seeing for all its olive groves even though there are fewer of them and they are less impressive than the magnificent giants on finds in the north.

In the past, the small bridge over Lefkimmi canal was the only route for Kavos. It is located in the approximate centre of Lefkimmi, which is called Potami as this where the river (*potami*) that ends in the sea passes (at the Bouka, as the locals say). The river effectively cuts Lefkimmi in two, and there are cafes and shops on both sides. The fishing boats that are moored here add a particularly charming touch to the whole scene.

Panoramic view of Lefkimmi from the Lefki belfry.

Kavos
Arkoudilas
Spartera

Asprokavos cape, Corfu's most southerly edge.

info

KAVOS

Type: A large beach over 3 km long with sands suitable for children.

Services: Sun umbrellas and recliners for hire. Restaurants with international and local cuisine, fast food many bars for hire along the beach, which are full day and night. There are various accommodation choices, such as a large number of hotels with swimming pools, rented rooms and apartments as well as a campsite. There are also all kinds of shops.

Activities: Water sports, boat trips, sea cycles and canoeing.

Features: Beloved destination for the under-30s but less attractive for those desiring a more restful holiday.

Going down the twisting road from Lefkimmi you follow the signs for Kavos (46 km.). This a village that has developed very rapidly because of its large and safe sand beach ideal for marine sports which are readily available there. You can also reach Kavos by turning off at Lefkimmi on the new road that leads to harbor of Lefkimmi which connected the area to Igoumenitsa opposite by ferry boat. Ai Prokopis celebrates its feast day on 8 July when there is a fair and, the evening before, a special church service with the participation of the metropolitan bishop and the Philharmonic Orchestra. **Arkoudilas** is the opposite of Kavos: a forest of cypress and mastic trees and arbutus shrubs, over a densely covered area of 25 hectares. A walk through its wildly sprouting vegetation is perfect at any time of day. The forest stops at a steep cliff edge over the sea, with a view that takes your breath away: cape Asprokavos. After the village of **Pantatika** you can make a choice between two roads: the one goes straight on and takes you to the southern most point of Corfu, **Cape Asprokavos** (where there is the small medival **Monastery of the Virgin Mary of Arkoudillas** and the one that goes to the right and ends up the village of Spartera (50 km.)The village is built on an elevation above th plain. Using the inland road and passing through the villages of **Dragotina, Palaiochori, Bastatika, Kritika** and **Niochori** you return to Lefkimmi.

You return to the crossroads at Vraganiotika and you turn left for Ayios Matthaios. Just before the village a turn left will take you to **Gardiki** from which there is a maze of roads leading off in all directions in that fertile area beneath the steep hill and north of the Koryssia salt lake. Gardiki has a Byzantine castle, the spitting image of the one at Angekokastro, built at almost exactly the same time and by the same Despotate of Epirus. It is octagonal, and was strongly reinforced by a tower at each corner. In the interior it is obvious that the builders used the remains of older buildings which can be seen built into the wall.

Agios Matthaios (22 km. from the town of Corfu). This is a large picturesque village, a curious mixture of the old and the new. Life has moved at its steady pace down through time but among the beautiful old houses there are also modern ones. One of the flagged lanes leads to the **Monastery of the Pantokrator** at the top of the hill. The church celebrates its feast day on 6 August, where there is a fine fair lasting into the night and which you should not miss. There is a cave there it is said has direct communications with the sea. Ayios Matthaios is enveloped in a true forest of olive trees.

On the road back to town you go through **Vouniatades** a village on the slopes of a hill with many beautiful old houses. The villages visible on your left are **Ano and Kato Pouliana**, which are characterised by their old stone houses and narrow neighbourhoods. On your left you pass the turn-off to **Kato Garouna**. The road remains rather high, above the beach, on the right hand side, with a very beautiful view of **Ai Gordis**. As you leave the village of Ayioi Theodori you see in front of you, the entire central section of the island, all the way to the town of Corfu. which is 12 km. away.

Gardiki
Agios Matthaios

Ruins of the Byzantine castle at Gardiki.

Halikounas

A sandy beach near Gardiki, over 10 km long, with very fine sands and waves that are perfect for surfing. It is right next to Korission lagoon, which is a protected Natura 2000 area, and there are thus no hotels or restaurants here. If you are thirsty or want to eat something, there is a Municipal canteen on the beach.

The mountain village of Agios Matthaios.

Achilleion
the refuge of the empress Elisabeth

Princess Elisabeth at a young age.

info

ACHILLEION
Opening hours:
Daily: 08:00-19:00.
Saturday, Sunday
08:00-14.30.
Information:
26610 56245.

The entrance to the Achilleion with the stairway.

Corfu, this beautiful mythical island of the Phaeceans has on ornament that is different than all the rest. It is special not so much for its beauty but rather for the people who created it or were connected to it, figures that were important to both world history and the history of Corfu itself. This is the Achilleio.

It was built at the end of the 19th century (1889-1891) by the queen of the Austro-Hungarian Empire, Elisabeth, better known as Sissi. It was purchased after her assassination by Kaiser William II of Germany. But the First World War that was started by him in 1914 and destroyed Germany prevented him from enjoying the Achilleio and Corfu. Perhaps if he had lived a little longer with the people of the Ionian, he would have come to understand the futility of his war within the beauty of nature and the power of time. The period that followed was a difficult one for this superb building and for all the areas that make it up.

The French occupation of the island, the Second World War, the island and the state economy that was in shambles at the end of the war led to the deterioration of the Achilleio.

Then, in 1962, the space was leased for twenty years to companies which under the expert guidance of a German baron began to restore the building, managing to get back many of the objects that has been sold or were presumed lost and the works of art that had ornamented it and set up a casino and the Achilleio Musseum which is still operating today. The casino has been transformed into one of the largest hotels on Corfu so that Achilles, Elisabeth and the Kaiser along with all the others who contributed to the creation of this space, can at last enjoy this jewel of the Ionian undisturbed.

Elisabeth and the Achilleio

Elisabeth was born in 1837 in Bavaria. Child of the Wittelsbach family, she was crowned the queen of Austria and Hungary, shortly after her scandalous marriage to Franz Joseph I of the Hapsburgs in 1854 since his wife was supposed to be the sister of Elisabeth, Elena. After her marriage Elisabeth who had already come into conflict with court protocol and her mother-in-law Sofia, started a series of trips. On one of these to Hungary in 1857 her daughter Sofia died at the age of two. At that time the mother-in-law who had already stated strong objections to those trips, attempted to gain guardianship of the two other children Elisabeth had at the time, Rudolph and Giselle. Elisabeth using her health as an excuse after all these developments began a long trip on a yacht throughout the islands of the Mediterranean. Thus in 1861 she arrived on Coru as the guest at Mon Repos of the English High Commissioner Sir Henry Storks.

Elizabeth at her coronation as Queen of Hungary. George Raab, Vienna, 1867.

Her first contact with the natural beauties of the island and the Ionian sea in general appear to have made a great impression on Elisabeth who on the many trips she was still to make she often stopped at Corfu slowly coming to know Greece, Greek history and mythology. But she herself though she played a positive role in the political developments in Europe in those areas of northern Italy and above all Hungary which was controlled by the Austrians, had to face, outside the hostile court, new personal tragedies as she lost her son Rudolf who committed suicide, and then her father, the Count Maximilian I who was executed in Mexico by the rebels under Benito (Pablo) Juarez, her cousin Ludwig II and her sister. After all these events Elisabeth decided to leave Austria and settle somewhere far away.

Her choice must have already begun to form in her mind after her first trip to Corfu in 1861. Thus in 1889 she purchasd the Villa Brailas which was then on the present-day site of the Achilleio and the work of tearing down the old and building the new builiding began. The work was completed in 1891, the decoration being done by Elisabeth herself.

The love that she developed for Greek mythology is clearly reflected in the name of the building and expresses her admiration for the greatest warrior of the Trojan War, Achilles. The superb garden that she created, decorated with marvellous works of sculpture, the main one being the Achilles Wounded. But Elisabeth did not manage to live for very long in her Achilleio dream palace. In 1898 while she was in Geneva she herself fell victim to the lengthy oppression of northern Italy by her empire. Luigi Luckeni, an Italian, stabbed her as she was coming out of her hotel. He himself was arrested and paid for his ideas by committing suicide in prison in 1910. That was the final epidoe of the much-discussd life of Elisabeth which with a great number of changes was finally made into a movie starring the famous Romy Schneider which appeared in 1955.

William II and the Achilleio

Kaiser Wilhelm II as a young man.

The second major figure who has a direct connection to the Achilleio was that of William II the German Kaiser who during his visit to Corfu in 1905 was a guest of the Greek royal family at the then royal estate of Mon Repos. He was then offered the chance to purchase the Achilleio which in fact did occur in 1907 after a series of negotiations. The character of the emperor who would start World War I (and would end up an exille in Denmark, condemned by history) made it impossible for him to look at such a great hero at the moment of his death, moved the statue of the Wounded Achilles to its present location and placed an order for the grand bronze Achilles that today dominates the area. This enormous statue, 11.5 meters high in all was brought to the locaton in sections and then assembled on its present site. The Kaiser also carried out other major works such as the erection of the observation post at Pelekas and the archaeological excavations that were begun at Ayioi Theodoroi.

The Achilleio and its History up to the Present

After the outbreak of World War I the Achilleio was abandoned by William II. In 1915 the French and Serbian forces which, with the assent from the Greek governor El. Venizelos, settled down in neutral Corfu, turned the building into a hospital.

As a result there was significant damage which was made even worse during World War II when the Achilleio was used by the Italian and German conquerors as a hospital and military headquarters. After the war the building was used to house schools, and a children's station.

Then in 1962 the Greek goverment funded a German company to repair the building with the aim of turning it into a casino. The President of the company Baron von Richthoffen, the third figure who is directly connected to the Achilleio, gathered together many of the objects that had been scattered here and there and returned a part of the building to a semblance of its original form.

With the end of the lease the building came back

into the hands of the Greek state to which it still belongs today while the casino has become one of the main hotels of the town of Corfu.

The most recent page in the long history of the Achilleio was written in 1994 when a summit conference of the leaders of the EEC was held there marking the end of the Greek presidentship. During the works that took place beforehand, the building and the grounds were given their presnt form and can thus narrate to the visitor its long and turbulent course down through time.

Exterior of the palace.

A TOUR OF THE ACHILLEIO

The **entrance** to the Achilleio buildng is through an iron gate whose name is written on the top part in Greek letters. Along the flagged pathway there are built-in triangular metal plaques on which are written the dates of the founding and the beginning of the erection of the building, 1889.

Next to the entrance is the building that houses the ticket office constructed during the same period. Right after that you take a path that leads to the facade of the building, and you see yet another building which was built during the Kaiser's time to house his own personal garrison and is called the **House of the Knights** while more recently it has been renovated and turned into the casino's guest-house.

Continuing on through the luxurious green **gardens** you come upon two statues which ornament the area. The first one on the right is "**The Musician with the Cymbals**" which is a bronze copy of an a ancient work which shows a young man with castanents on his hands and another percussion instrument on his right foot at the moment he is playing. This beautiful sculpture is followed by a newer one both in age and technique done by a marble sculptor whose name is no longer known. **This is the "Future Sailor"** a young man who is sitting on the stern of a broken-down boat and wearing a sailor's cap from the time, is studying the atlas.

Just before you reach the road along the facade of the building there is another bronze statue, a copy of the one in the Capitalium of Rome which in its turn is a copy of a work by Lysippos. This is a **Hermes**, which was originally in the place that is occupied by Achilles Wounded.

You are now at the **facade of the Achilleio**. The facade of the building is full of sculpture and reliefs with subjects taken from ancient Greek mythology. On the balcony on the first floor there are two imposing marble centaurs, the older one to the left and the younger one to the right. On the second floor balcony there are four bronze Muses with four torches raised on high which today contain electric lighting. On the left side of the veranda of the second floor three is also a bronze winged Hermes who is holding a proclamation. On the right side of the facade there is another building which housed the stables and their personnel. Later is was used as a garrison during various wars and then was used as a school during the period between the wars. In 1962 it was repaired and became the residence of Baron von Richthoffen. Later over the entrance to the Achilleio a plaque was set up which states that in 1914 during World War I the French forces were housed there.

The musician with the cymbals.

The large iron door was built by the Caponetti Compnay in Naples Italy. It is decorated with relief gryphons and Meduses, lions and halcyons as well as two bronze depictions in relief, to the left there is Zeus who in his cheriot is sending a thunderbolt against the Titans and to the right the chariot of the Titan Ilios.

The columns that support the first floor balcony are done in the Doric style. The area in front of the entrance was enclosed with glass by William II and was later used by the French and Serb forces as a mortuary. This glassed in area was removed during the repars that were done to the building and has now been restored to its original form.

In the main reception area your attention is taken by the staircaes that leads to the upper floors, with their impressive and ornate bronze railings. At their base are two statues, one of Zeus and his thunderbolt to the right and another of Hra with a peacock to left. Then as one goes up the stairs there are many small bronze statues with mythological figures such as the Selenoi, Maenads, Satyrs, Bacchoi, Meduses and Caryatids as well as lions.

As the bases of the ceiling there are plaster of Paris sculptures of Artemis, Phoibus Apollo, Aphrodite and Hermes which are located on the mezzanine section while on the first floor their are ancient trophies and on the second Pan and his entourage all, done by the Caponetti Company, works by Filippo Eugemnio.

In front of the staircase you can see two Doric columns and next to them two copies of ancient kraters with mythological representations, made of Florentine porcelain. To your left there is a superb marble fireplace made of marbe from Porto Verente in Italy, two statuettes, of Athena Pallas to the right and Hebe to the left. In the middle there is a clock from the time of Elisabeth. Right of the main entrance there is an engraved portrait of Elisabeth at the age of 21, a copy that

The marvellous work "
The Four Seasons" on the ceiling of the reception hall.

was done by Luis Jacoby from the orginal done by the German painter Winterhalter which is the Hofburg Palace.

On the ceiling of this reception area of the Achilleio there has been preserved a marvellous work by a painter with the pseudonym Callopi called **"The Four Seasons"** which are symbolized by women with grapes that stand for the Fall, women before the fire in Winter, children with flowers that show it is Spring and small angels or cupids with shells to show that is it is summer. In the upper part of the picture the Hours, the daughters of Zeus, are dancing against the sky. The painting decoration around the picture is done in the Pompey style, a copy of the finds from Pompey.

The Side-Chapel of the Achilleio

Elisabeth created to the right of the entrance a Catholic chapel which contains important works of eccelsiastical art. In the cupola there is a wall painting of the Judgment of Jesus of exceptional beauty and below this a large painting of the Virgin Mary by Franz Matsch which Elisabeth called "The Star of the Sea" in reference to a tempest in which she herself was in danger on one of her voyages on her yacht. Right and left there two statues, of the Virgin Mary and Jesus Christ, and the entire cupola is supported on Corinthian style columns.

The Holy Altar still exists and the oratory as well as other important objects the main ones being the vestments that were donated to Elisabeth by Pope Pius IX.

On the walls there are important and semi-relief representations made of marble, alabaster and majolica and the decoration is supplemented by a life-like image of the Virgin Mary from the Gardens of Marseilles and portraits of Roman Catholic and Greek Orthodox hierarchs.

Personal Articles Belonging to Elisabeth and William

Here are on exhibit are objects and documents that pertain to the personal life of Elisabeth. Among the items on display are some special photographs of her and the members of her family, paintings as well as photographs of the Achilleio from that period. There is also an album of the Hapsburg family as well as documents that are related to her assassination in Geneva.

Smoking Room Dining Room

In this space, where items related to the German emperor are on display, the things of especial interest, besides the paintings and the photographs that have historical value, are a saddle which he used, many small objects, a small model of his yacht which was a naval marvel during its time as well as the ship's flag.

The first room to the left of the entrance, which today houses the Museum's offices, was originally the smoking room of the Achilleio, right next to the dining room which today have on display objects and furniture from the former owners. There are also important paintings here as well as the sword with which Franz Joseph I was defeated by Napoleon III of France. The ceilings and the walls are lavishly decorated although only a part of the original decoration has survived. Contuing on you come to a small space which was created during the renovation of the building in 1962 and today contains five marble reliefs, copies of ancient works with subjects taken from Greek mythology as well as from Sappho, the "tenth muse" of ancient Greek lyric poetry.

In the final two rooms of the Achilleio Museum the furniture of Elisabeth is on display as well as various items belonging to William II. In the first space is the desk and a significant amount of furniture of the Austrian queen, a bookcase with books from the same period and photographs of the German Kaiser and other officials. There is also a royal crown on display, jewellery and many copies of statues from the Vatican Museum and Naples.

In the second room can be seen the furniture from Elisabeth's bedroom, two wardrobes and mirrors, and a couch - a copy of the corresponding Roman ones, a desk as well as an Arab amphora decorated with gold and enamel which was given as a gift to William. There is also an excellent painting in this area by Ludwig Thiersch called "Odysseus and Nausicaa".

First and Second Rooms of Furniture

Various shots of the rooms with the furniture.

This magnificent oil painting, a work by Franz Matsch lies at the top of the staircase which leads from the reception area. It depicts the dragging of the dead Hector around the walls of Troy by the triumphant Achilles. According to Homer when Achilles withdrew from fighting the Trojans because of his dispute with Agamemnon, his friend Patroclos asked for his armor so that he could go into battle. Because since the time that Achilles stopped fighting the Trojans had driven the Greeks to their ships quite a number of times. Achilles agreed but with the condition that he not be lured to the walls of Troy. Indeed, the armor of Achilles and his chariot terrified the Trojans who withdrew and thus without realizing it Patroclos reached the gates of Troy. But Hector, who was standing before him, killed him and took his panoply and while he also killed his charioteer the horses of Achilles returned by themselves to the camp. After many hours of battle when the Greeks were finally able to take back the dead body of Patroclos, Achilles prepared his revenge.

He ordered new weapons and panoply from his mother Thetis, which was made for him by Hephaestus. From that moment on he waited to find Hector which would be unavoidable in the coming battles. In their ensuing clash, just as Apollo had first struck Patroclos, thus Athena now confusd Hector who in the end fell down dead struck in the throat by Achilles' spear. Afterwards, and after all the Achaeans had driven their lances into the dead body of Hector, Achilles dragged his body around the walls of Troy three times tied to his cheriot. This scene has been immortalized by the creator of the work.

The Triumph of Achilles

Vase from Sissi's bedroom.

'The Triumph of Achilles'
by Franz Matsch.

There are also some other important details in the work. The body of the dead Hector despite having been pierced by the spears of all the Greeks, remained untouched. This happended because Apollo did not want such a thing to occur to someone who had been protected by him.

Furthermore, at the gates of Troy, on the lintel there is a swastika. This is a very ancient symbol whose origins are from some unknown site in the East, the swastika was among other things one of the symbols of Troy.

Finally, one can see how while the painting is full of motion, the wheel of Achilles' chariot appears to be motionless. According to one thiory this was a deliberate "mistake" of the creator who was using the reasoning prevalent during the chariot races of the Roman period. There is, of course, the rumor, that the artist committed suicide becuse of this failure.

The Gardens of the Achilleio

Going outside, at the end of the staircase, you find yourslf at the entrance to the gardens of the Achilleio. You are officially "met" by four marble statues, of Aphrodite and Artemis down below and Hermes and Apollo at the end of the short staircase. The grove of the Achilleio, the peristyle of the Muses, the stoa of the wisemen, the landscaping of the gardens, are full of marbleand bronze statues, copies of ancient works in the main but with a number of original creations.

It is worth looking at them one by one but also to view the site as an aesthetic whole which takes us back to the lavish aesthetics of the 19th century.

Of the statues, except for the Wounded Achilles and the Achilles Triumphant, which we have just described, there is the exceptional Phryni by Fritz Heinemann, this famous courtesan who during antiquity was the model for Praxiteles, because of her exceptionally beautiful body. Indeed her beauty was such that it convinced an entire court to let her go free when she stood naked before it. Also of interest, but unfortunately not open to the general public, is the statue of Elisabeth which is located at the old entrance to the Achilleio, to the grove. A photograph of the statue is on display in the museum.

The Muses' peristyle.

The Wounded Achilles

This is the most important statue in the Achillieio and was dearly treasured by its first owner, Elisabeth. It is a work by the German sculptor Gustav Herter done in 1884 and was transferred to Corfu with the completion of works during the erection of the building.

The work shows us Achilles, the gratests of the Achaean warriors, after he has been mortally wounded in the heel by an arrow. According to Homer, the mother of Achilles, who was an immortal herself, also wanted to make her son immortal. Thus acting without the knowledge of Peleas, her mortal husband, she burned the small Achilles every night and then dipped him into the

water of the Styx river so that he would become invincible. Only his heel, which she held him by, was not invincible. Knowing this Apollo sent a message to Paris where to aim his bow and arrow at Achilles from afar. Th arrow, which the god himself sent on its way, hit its target and Achliles, as is depicted in relief here, is making an attempt to pull it from the wound.

Achilles Triumphant

This death scene of Achilles was not at all liked by the second owner of the Achilleio, William II. That is why he orderd it be set up in the place where the "Wounded Achilles" was originally found. This majestic bronze statue is still in the same place today. Its creator was the German Johann Gotz. The statue is rather mediocre from an artistic point of view but it does express the predominate spirit in the Germany of that time. At the base of the statue there was, in line with ancient models, an inscription from ancient Greek that said "This statue of Achilles, son of Peleas was erected here by William of the powerful Germans so that he will be remembered by those who are to come". This inscription was removed by the French during World War I.

The Wounded Achilles.

Achilles Triumphant.

Paxoi - Antipaxoi
Diapontian Islands
Ereikoussas, Mathraki, Othonoi

Introduction

Nature which gave Corfu so many beautiful ornaments also granted it some other priceless gifts scatttered throughout the Ionian sea.

These are the small islets which surround it,the legendary Scheria, Paxoi and Antipaxoi to the southeast, the Diapontia islands to the northwest each have their own way of life, their own legends and history which they will reveal to all those who wander along their tranquil and sparkling clean beaches, through their lush olive groves and their small fishing harbors.

Opposite page:
Gaios, the impressive capital of Paxoi.

Right: Paxoi rocks.
Below: Kipous beach, Paxoi.

PAXOI
Gaios

Gaios, which is also the capital of the island has an impressive harbor. There are two islets with dense vegetation which stand before it. The one is **Panayia** with a monastery of the same name and the other **Ai-Nikolas** which forms a picturesque little fjord with the mainland opposite. There is a Venetian castle and a windmill on Ai-Nikolas. Gaios took its name from disciple of the Apostle Paul who brought Christianity to the Paxians, died and was buried there. The houses of Gaios, which have preserved their traditional Ionian Island architecture, the narrow alleyways with their tiny shops, the bars and the cafes create a light-hearted atmosphere. Right next to the harbor are the Historical Archives, the Library, and the church of the Ayioi Apostoloi (Holy Apostles) with wall paintings. There are two small beaches southeast of the harbor. From Gaios there is one road that crosses the island from south to north passing through olive groves.

Longos - Lakka

At a distance of 5.5 km. north of Gaios, to the back of a small bay, is the village of Longos nestled in greenery. At the end of the road one reaches Lakka another picturesque village at the back of sheltered bay. Near Lakka is the beautiful sand beach of Charamis and the Byzantine church of the Ypapantis (Candlemas).

A Tour Round the Island by Caique

Opposite page:
Above: The little harbour of Lakka.
Centre: Longos, the little beach village of Paxoi.
Below: Aerial photograph of Gaios.

Setting off from Gaios and heading southeast you will reach the coast of **Ozias** near the islets of Mongonisi and Kaltsionisi. You will subsequntly see **Trypytos**, a natural stone bridge, the cliffs of **Mousmoulis** the **cave of Ortholithos** with the enormous monolith called Ermitis at its entrance. The **cave of Kastanida** at the base of a cliff 180 m. high and finally the **cave of Ypapantis**, a refuge for seals.

ANTIPAXOI

This small island is only three miles from Gaios on Paxos. On this small piece of land, only 5 sq. km, with its handful of residents you will find the finest sand beaches, the most luminous of blue seas and naturally enough the cleanest water.

You will come to Agrapidia, you will swim at Voutoumi and Vrika and then stroll up through the vineyards to see the view from high up. During the summer there are caiques every day from Paxoi and Corfu to Antipaxoi.

DIAPONTIA ISLANDS

A short distance (3-7 nautical miles) from Sidari on Corfu there are three verdant little islands with beautiful sand beaches and crystal clear water, Ereikousa, Marthaki and Othonoi, known as the Diapontia islands. They have a total aeram of no more than 18 sq. km. and the total number of inhabitants on each of them is around 200. Generally speaking their history was the same as that of neighboring Corfu which they always belonged to and on which they were completely dependent.

But isolated as they are it is equally certain they were constantly being attackd by pirates whom they were unable to defend themselves against. Many believe that Othonoi, the largest island, is the island of Calypso, the Ogygia of Homer. Where Odysseus was shipwrecked and went to find refuge. A cave, 20 minutes from the harbor, is said to be the legandery cave of the nymph who kept the man for seven whole years on the island.

Voutourni beach,
one of Antipaxoi's many beaches.

Texts: Katerina Tsouxtidi
Art direction: Evi Damiri
Image processing: Giorgos Paraskevas
Cover design: Panagiotis Smyrnis
Photographs: M. Toubis Archives

Printing and Productions: M. Toubis Editions SA